T0311399

An Analysis of

Adam Smith's
The Wealth of Nations

By
John Collins

Published by Macat International Ltd
24:13 Coda Centre, 189 Munster Road, London SW6 6AW.

Distributed exclusively by Routledge
2 Park Square, Milton Park, Abingdon, Oxon OX14 4RN
711 Third Avenue, New York, NY 10017, USA

Routledge is an imprint of the Taylor & Francis Group, an informa business

Copyright © 2017 by Macat International Ltd
Macat International has asserted its right under the Copyright, Designs and Patents Act
1988 to be identified as the copyright holder of this work.

The print publication is protected by copyright. Prior to any prohibited reproduction, storage in
a retrieval system, distribution or transmission in any form or by any means, electronic, mechanical, recording or otherwise, permission should be obtained from the publisher or where
applicable a license permitting restricted copying in the United Kingdom should be obtained
from the Copyright Licensing Agency Ltd, Barnard's Inn, 86 Fetter Lane, London EC4A 1EN, UK.

The ePublication is protected by copyright and must not be copied, reproduced, transferred,
distributed, leased, licensed or publicly performed or used in any way except as specifically
permitted in writing by the publishers, as allowed under the terms and conditions under which
it was purchased, or as strictly permitted by applicable copyright law. Any unauthorised distribution or use of this text may be a direct infringement of the authors and the publishers' rights
and those responsible may be liable in law accordingly.

www.macat.com
info@macat.com

Cataloguing in Publication Data
A catalogue record for this book is available from the British Library.
Library of Congress Cataloguing-in-Publication Data is available upon request.
Cover illustration: Etienne Gilfillan

ISBN 978-1-912302-31-4 (hardback)
ISBN 978-1-912127-08-5 (paperback)
ISBN 978-1-912281-19-0 (e-book)

Notice
The information in this book is designed to orientate readers of the work under analysis,
to elucidate and contextualise its key ideas and themes, and to aid in the development
of critical thinking skills. It is not meant to be used, nor should it be used, as a
substitute for original thinking or in place of original writing or research. References and
notes are provided for informational purposes and their presence does not constitute
endorsement of the information or opinions therein. This book is presented solely for
educational purposes. It is sold on the understanding that the publisher is not engaged
to provide any scholarly advice. The publisher has made every effort to ensure that
this book is accurate and up-to-date, but makes no warranties or representations with
regard to the completeness or reliability of the information it contains. The information
and the opinions provided herein are not guaranteed or warranted to produce particular
results and may not be suitable for students of every ability. The publisher shall not be
liable for any loss, damage or disruption arising from any errors or omissions, or from
the use of this book, including, but not limited to, special, incidental, consequential or
other damages caused, or alleged to have been caused, directly or indirectly, by the
information contained within.

CONTENTS

THE MACAT LIBRARY

The Macat Library is a series of unique academic explorations of seminal works in the humanities and social sciences – books and papers that have had a significant and widely recognised impact on their disciplines. It has been created to serve as much more than just a summary of what lies between the covers of a great book. It illuminates and explores the influences on, ideas of, and impact of that book. Our goal is to offer a learning resource that encourages critical thinking and fosters a better, deeper understanding of important ideas.

Each publication is divided into three Sections: Influences, Ideas, and Impact. Each Section has four Modules. These explore every important facet of the work, and the responses to it.

This Section-Module structure makes a Macat Library book easy to use, but it has another important feature. Because each Macat book is written to the same format, it is possible (and encouraged!) to cross-reference multiple Macat books along the same lines of inquiry or research. This allows the reader to open up interesting interdisciplinary pathways.

To further aid your reading, lists of glossary terms and people mentioned are included at the end of this book (these are indicated by an asterisk [*] throughout) – as well as a list of works cited.

Macat has worked with the University of Cambridge to identify the elements of critical thinking and understand the ways in which six different skills combine to enable effective thinking.
Three allow us to fully understand a problem; three more give us the tools to solve it. Together, these six skills make up the **PACIER** model of critical thinking. They are:

ANALYSIS – understanding how an argument is built
EVALUATION – exploring the strengths and weaknesses of an argument
INTERPRETATION – understanding issues of meaning

CREATIVE THINKING – coming up with new ideas and fresh connections
PROBLEM-SOLVING – producing strong solutions
REASONING – creating strong arguments

To find out more, visit **WWW.MACAT.COM.**

CRITICAL THINKING AND *THE WEALTH OF NATIONS*

Primary critical thinking skill: REASONING
Secondary critical thinking skill: CREATIVE THINKING

Adam Smith's 1776 Inquiry into *The Nature and Causes of the Wealth of Nations* – more often known simply as *The Wealth of Nations* – is one of the most important books in modern intellectual history.

Considered one of the fundamental works of classical economics, it is also a prime example of the enduring power of good reasoning, and the ability of reasoning to drive critical thinking forward. Adam Smith was attempting to answer two complex questions: where does a nation's wealth come from, and what can governments do to increase it most efficiently? At the time, perhaps the most widely accepted theory, mercantilism, argued that a nation's wealth was literally the amount of gold and silver it held in reserve. Smith, meanwhile, weighed the evidence and came to a different conclusion: a nation's wealth, he argued, lay in its ability to encourage economic activity, largely without government interference.

Underlying this radical redefinition was the revolutionary concept that powered Smith's reasoning and which continues to exert a vast influence on economic thought: the idea that markets are self-regulating. Pitting his arguments against those of his predecessors, Smith carefully and persuasively reasoned out a strong case for free markets that reshaped government economic policies in the 19th-century and continues to shape global prosperity today.

ABOUT THE AUTHOR OF THE ORIGINAL WORK

Adam Smith is known as the "father of modern economics." Born in Kircaldy, Scotland, in 1723, he studied moral philosophy and went on to lecture in logic. His first book, *The Theory of Moral Sentiments*, explores the question of morality. His second, *An Inquiry into the Nature and Causes of the Wealth of Nations* (often just called *The Wealth of Nations*), asks how societies accumulate wealth and how that wealth is used. In this book, Smith supports the idea of free trade with minimum government intervention. *The Wealth of Nations* was an instant success, and his ideas have since been debated internationally, and have had a huge impact on government policy, as well as altering the nature of global trade relationships. Smith died in 1790, but, more than 200 years later, his ideas live on.

ABOUT THE AUTHOR OF THE ANALYSIS

Dr John Collins is a member of the faculty at the London School of Economics, where he is currently Executive Director of the LSE IDEAS International Drug Policy Project.

ABOUT MACAT

GREAT WORKS FOR CRITICAL THINKING

Macat is focused on making the ideas of the world's great thinkers accessible and comprehensible to everybody, everywhere, in ways that promote the development of enhanced critical thinking skills.

It works with leading academics from the world's top universities to produce new analyses that focus on the ideas and the impact of the most influential works ever written across a wide variety of academic disciplines. Each of the works that sit at the heart of its growing library is an enduring example of great thinking. But by setting them in context – and looking at the influences that shaped their authors, as well as the responses they provoked – Macat encourages readers to look at these classics and game-changers with fresh eyes. Readers learn to think, engage and challenge their ideas, rather than simply accepting them.

'Macat offers an amazing first-of-its-kind tool for interdisciplinary learning and research. Its focus on works that transformed their disciplines and its rigorous approach, drawing on the world's leading experts and educational institutions, opens up a world-class education to anyone.'

Andreas Schleicher
Director for Education and Skills, Organisation for Economic Co-operation and Development

'Macat is taking on some of the major challenges in university education … They have drawn together a strong team of active academics who are producing teaching materials that are novel in the breadth of their approach.'

Prof Lord Broers,
former Vice-Chancellor of the University of Cambridge

'The Macat vision is exceptionally exciting. It focuses upon new modes of learning which analyse and explain seminal texts which have profoundly influenced world thinking and so social and economic development. It promotes the kind of critical thinking which is essential for any society and economy. This is the learning of the future.'

Rt Hon Charles Clarke, former UK Secretary of State for Education

'The Macat analyses provide immediate access to the critical conversation surrounding the books that have shaped their respective discipline, which will make them an invaluable resource to all of those, students and teachers, working in the field.'

Professor William Tronzo, University of California at San Diego

WAYS IN TO THE TEXT

KEY POINTS

- A pioneering figure in the history of economic theory, Adam Smith was born in the Scottish town of Kircaldy in 1723.

- *The Wealth of Nations* offers a framework for understanding the operations of the free-market economy*—an economy that functions with minimal government intervention.

- Smith's book became a foundational text in the study of economics. It remains a highly relevant work.

Who Was Adam Smith?

Adam Smith, the author of *The Wealth of Nations* (1776), was born in the Scottish town of Kircaldy in June 1723. His father, also Adam Smith, was a solicitor, a prosecutor, and the "comptroller of the customs" in his local town.[1] He died two months after his son's birth. Smith's mother, Margaret Douglas, did not remarry. She raised her son,[2] sending him to a local school between 1729 and 1737 where he received a strong grounding in mathematics, Latin, and history. Then, at the age of 14, Smith began studies at the University of Glasgow. He studied moral philosophy* (the philosophy of ethics and moral behavior) under the Irish Scottish philosopher Francis Hutcheson,* who became a formative influence.[3] Smith's time in Glasgow gave him a grounding in many of the liberal* and Enlightenment* ideas he developed in his later academic career ("liberalism" is a philosophy grounded in ideas of freedom and equality; "the Enlightenment" of the late 1600s to the late 1700s was an influential period of European intellectual history that emphasized rational thought and individuality).

In 1740 Smith joined Balliol College, Oxford, but he was unhappy there and returned to Scotland before completing his scholarship.[4] By 1748, he was giving lectures in Edinburgh in which he began to elaborate his own ideas: a synthesis of philosophy and economic thought. He also began to discuss his views on the importance of individual freedom: his "system of natural liberty."[5] In 1751 Smith received a professorship at Glasgow University, teaching logic. Eight years later he published his first book, *The Theory of Moral Sentiments*,[6] which brought him international recognition as a thinker. His second work, *The Wealth of Nations,* was published in 1776 and was enormously successful.[7] Smith subsequently took up a position as commissioner of customs in Scotland and lived in Edinburgh until his death in 1790 at the age of 67.[8]

What Does *The Wealth of Nations* Say?

The Wealth of Nations provides a framework for understanding the market economy*—an economy founded on the principle of supply and demand. Smith argues that the free market (a market that operates without government interference) is not a chaotic or problematic form of economic life, but actually produces optimal outcomes. It does this as a consequence of individuals pursuing their own self-interest. This idea—that within the market, individual self-interest promotes a functioning and efficient system beneficial to society—is key to what is known as the "classical"* school of economics. *The Wealth of Nations* was a foundational text for this school.

Classical economists argued that markets are fundamentally self-regulating and self-correcting—but only if they are free from government interference and if individuals are free from coercion.

Under these conditions, as Smith describes it, markets appear to be governed by an "invisible hand"* that produces a natural stability: supply meets demand and resources are used effectively. Competition is a vital component of this system; market equilibrium can only be reached if buyers can choose between various suppliers. Then suppliers can compete for buyers, and companies that do not win buyers are allowed to fail. Smith warns repeatedly of the dangers of monopoly,* where one firm controls supply.

Overall, *The Wealth of Nations* provides a systematic way of understanding capitalism* (the dominant political and social ideology of the West, in which industry is held in private hands) and the market economy. It also provides an insight into how a "free-market" ideology forms. A free-market approach to economics views the competitive market as "natural." As such, it is best left free from government interference. These arguments have tremendous resonance in contemporary society. Today's political and economic debates usually fit somewhere on a spectrum, advocating either more or less government interference. For example, in the United States, the Tea Party* is a conservative political grouping that advocates minimal government intervention. They see a vision of the society they want in the ideas of Smith and classical economics. Meanwhile, the largest center-left party in the United States, the Democratic Party,* is not ideologically opposed to government intervention. It generally rejects Smith's notion that the "invisible hand" creates equilibrium in an unregulated free market, and argues that the free market is detrimental to those who are less well off; it believes that social justice is achieved through government policies that consider the well-being of this section of society.

When the communist* Soviet Union* collapsed in 1991, many believed that this represented the triumph of free-market capitalism and the death of alternative forms of economic life.[9] There was a rush toward freer markets and trade around the globe. Adherence to Smith's ideas appeared set in stone. But this view was challenged by the global financial crisis of 2007–8* and the subsequent recession. These upheavals led to the reemergence of the debates about government oversight of the economy and the free market. These are the debates that began in earnest with Adam Smith and *The Wealth of Nations.*

Why Does *The Wealth of Nations* Matter?

Smith's text has as much relevance, if not more, today as it did when it was published. The key questions asked in *The Wealth of Nations* still preoccupy us. What is the role of the government in the economy? What outcomes may be expected if individuals are left to interact freely within the free market? What is the best way to organize society? Why, in all the apparent chaos of the world, is there a seeming order to socioeconomic life?

When Smith was writing the book, he was arguing against the dominant economic paradigm, or model, of eighteenth-century Europe: that of mercantilism.* According to this theory, a nation's economy exists only as a way to strengthen the government—in which case it should be strongly controlled by the state. Mercantilism also held that a nation's wealth is determined by the stock of gold and silver physically present within it, so the role of government is to prevent these commodities from leaving the country; a nation can hang on to its wealth by imposing high tariffs on imports and by protecting national industries and agriculture.

After the publication of *The Wealth of Nations*, in which Smith successfully challenged mercantilism, the theory went into a steep decline. Governments, particularly that of Britain, began pursuing global free-trade policies. Bolstered by the policies of the British Empire, the modern globalized world (that is, a world characterized by economic, political, and cultural ties across borders and oceans) came more strongly into view throughout the nineteenth century.

More than two centuries after *The Wealth of* Nations was published, governments around the world still address many of the issues discussed within it. The massive expansion of global trade and the constant efforts to diminish barriers to trade reveal the strength of free-trade ideas. The existence and influence of the World Trade Organization,* a global institution based in Switzerland that addresses the rules of international trade, is a clear example of this. While the most powerful states in the world remain committed to international trade, questions about the role of governments within the economy continue to be asked—as do questions about the effectiveness of the free market. Following Smith, classical economists argue that markets are preferable to government intervention and should be left to their own devices.[10] Meanwhile, other economists argue that the market is fundamentally unstable; they call for greater government oversight and regulation of the economy, and state management of supply and demand.[11]

NOTES

1   John Rae, *Life of Adam Smith* (London: MacMillan, 1895), 1.

2   Marie Bussing-Burks, *Influential Economists* (Minneapolis: The Oliver Press, 2003), 38–9.

3   Bussing-Burks, *Influential Economists*, 39.

4   Bussing-Burks, *Influential Economists*, 42.

5   Bussing-Burks, *Influential Economists*, 43.

6   Adam Smith, *The Theory of Moral Sentiments*, edited by Knud Haakonssen (Cambridge: Cambridge University Press, 2002 (New Rochelle, NY: Arlington House, 1969).

7   James Buchan, *The Authentic Adam Smith: His Life and Ideas* (New York: W. W. Norton & Co, 2006), 90.

8   Buchan, *The Authentic Adam Smith*, 145.

9   Francis Fukuyama, *The End of History and the Last Man*, 1st ed. (New York: Maxwell Macmillan International, 1992).

10 Milton Friedman and Rose D. Friedman, *Capitalism and Freedom*, 40th ed. (Chicago, IL: University of Chicago Press, 2002).

11 Paul Krugman, *End This Depression Now!* (New York: W. W. Norton & Co, 2013).

SECTION 1
INFLUENCES

MODULE 1
THE AUTHOR AND THE
HISTORICAL CONTEXT

KEY POINTS

- *The Wealth of Nations* is generally considered to be one of the most important works in the history of ideas.

- Adam Smith was born in Scotland, where he underwent his most formative education before moving to study at Oxford—an experience he did not enjoy.

- In 1776 Adam Smith published *The Wealth of Nations*, which became synonymous with his contribution to the study of economics.

Why Read This Text?

Adam Smith published his greatest work, *An Inquiry into the Nature and Causes of the Wealth of Nations* (usually abbreviated to *The Wealth of Nations*), in 1776. It had a tremendous influence on academic discourses at the time of publication and has informed debates about politics and economics ever since. The book became the founding text for the field of economics, with the former chairman of the US Federal Reserve,* Alan Greenspan,* describing it as "one of the greatest achievements in human intellectual history."[1] It is for this reason that all students of economics (and indeed scholars in the field of politics, history, and other branches of social sciences and the humanities) need to engage with Smith's ideas and work. He remains one of the key figures of the European Enlightenment,* the philosophical movement that emerged in Europe during the late seventeenth century and emphasized the importance of rational thought. Smith's arguments about the importance of individual liberty mean he also remains one of the greatest liberal* theorists of all time.

> ❝ In his *Wealth of Nations*, Smith reached far beyond the insights of his predecessors to frame a global view of how market economies, just then emerging, worked. In so doing, he supported changes in societal organization that were to measurably enhance world standards of living. ❞
>
> Alan Greenspan,* "Adam Smith"

Smith's central insight in *The Wealth of Nations* is that participants in the economic sphere can produce economic stability and positive socioeconomic outcomes simply by pursuing their own rational self-interest. As Smith writes: "It is not from the benevolence of the butcher, the brewer, or the baker, that we expect our dinner, but from their regard to their own interest."[2] This insight became the basis for modern economics. It lies at the heart of modern belief about the efficiency of the free market*—a market that operates with the very minimum of government intervention.

Author's Life

Adam Smith was born in the Scottish town of Kirkaldy in June 1723. His father, Adam Smith, a solicitor, died two months after his son was born. Smith's mother, Margaret Douglas, was the daughter of Scottish landed gentry and did not remarry after her husband's death.[3] Smith had a close relationship with his mother and it is generally believed, despite a lack of biographical material about his early life, that she encouraged his academic pursuits. He had a private tutor before starting at a local school in 1729. In 1737, aged 14, Smith began studying moral philosophy*—inquiry into the nature of ethics and ethical action—at the University of Glasgow, under the Scottish Irish philosopher Francis Hutcheson.*[4] This experience gave him a grounding in many of the liberal and Enlightenment ideas he would develop in his later academic career.

In 1740 Smith joined Balliol College, Oxford. He was not happy there, preferring the academic freedoms and stimulus of Scotland. In *The Wealth of Nations* he famously wrote: "In the University of Oxford, the greater part of the public professors have, for these many years, given up altogether even the pretence of teaching."[5] Elsewhere he recounts how he was punished for reading the work of the contemporary Scottish philosopher David Hume.*[6] Smith eventually started to suffer a nervous breakdown and left Oxford in 1746, before completing his scholarship.[7]

But two years on he began giving lectures in Edinburgh. These covered a range of topics, including the art of rhetoric and language, and were sponsored by the Philosophical Society of Edinburgh.*[8] It was during these lectures that Smith started to elaborate his synthesis of philosophy and economic thought, exploring, in particular, "the obvious and simple system of natural liberty."[9] Then, in 1751, he received a professorship at Glasgow University, teaching courses in logic. Two years later he became head of moral philosophy at the university.[10] He was to continue working as an academic for 13 years, describing this as "the happiest and most honorable period" of his life.[11]

Author's Background

Smith published his first book, *The Theory of Moral Sentiments,*[12] in 1759. This was a time of great upheaval in Europe as the old social and economic structures appeared to be breaking down. While an emerging merchant class was seeking to increase its economic freedom and foster upward social mobility, kings and the aristocracy sought to maintain the status quo, notably by securing their control over the economy. The merchant class wanted to break free from traditional social structures in which individuals were born into a position and remained in it for the rest of their lives. Writing against this backdrop, Smith argues in *The Theory of Moral Sentiments* that the economy could function without strict government control.

The book made Smith internationally famous. Students traveled to Glasgow from other countries to study under him.[13] It was then that Smith began to shift his emphasis from morality to the study of laws and economics, and resigned from teaching at the University of Glasgow to take on private tutoring; this allowed him to travel through Europe and meet leading figures of the European Enlightenment such as the French philosopher Voltaire* and the French economist François Quesnay.* He was also able to earn far more—roughly twice what he earned as a lecturer.[14] The experience had a profound influence on Smith's work. When the tutoring ended in 1766 he returned home to Kirkaldy in Scotland and spent most of the next decade writing *The Wealth of Nations*. This was eventually published in 1776, meeting with enormous success.[15]

Smith subsequently took up a position as commissioner of customs in Scotland and lived in Edinburgh until his death in 1790.[16]

NOTES

1   Alan Greenspan, "Remarks by Chairman Alan Greenspan: Adam Smith," The Federal Reserve Board, February 6, 2005, accessed October 16, 2015, http://www.federalreserve.gov/boarddocs/speeches/2005/20050206/default.htm

2   Adam Smith, *An Inquiry into the Nature and Causes of the Wealth of Nations: Books I, II, III, IV and V* (New York: Metalibri Digital Edition, 2007), 16. Accessed October 16, 2015. http://www.ibiblio.org/ml/libri/s/SmithA_WealthNations_p.pdf

3   Marie Bussing-Burks, *Influential Economists*, (Minneapolis: The Oliver Press, 2003), 38–9.

4   Bussing-Burks, *Influential Economists*, 39.

5   Smith, *The Wealth of Nations*, 589.

6   Todd Buchholz, *New Ideas from Dead Economists: An Introduction to Modern Economic Thought* (London: Penguin Books, 1999), 12.

7   Bussing-Burks, *Influential Economists*, 42.

8 John Rae, *Life of Adam Smith*, (London: MacMillan, 1895), 30.

9 Bussing-Burks, *Influential Economists*, 43.

10 Bussing-Burks, *Influential Economists*, 43.

11 Rae, *Life of Adam Smith*, 42.

12 Adam Smith, *The Theory of Moral Sentiments*, edited by Knud Haakonssen (Cambridge: Cambridge University Press, 2002).

13 Buchholz, *New ideas from Dead Economists*, 15.

14 Bucholz, *New Ideas from Dead Economists*, 16.

15 James Buchan, *The Authentic Adam Smith: His Life and Ideas* (New York: W. W. Norton & Co, 2006), 90.

16 Buchan, *The Authentic Adam Smith*, 145.

MODULE 2
ACADEMIC CONTEXT

KEY POINTS

- Adam Smith published *The Wealth of Nations* at a time of rapid socioeconomic change.

- Smith's economic ideas were influenced by the theories of the French physiocrats*—thinkers who argued that a nation's wealth is based on its agricultural wealth.

- Smith disliked mercantilism*—an economic theory founded on the belief that the role of the economy is to strengthen the national government.

The Work in Its Context

When Adam Smith wrote *The Wealth of Nations*, the field of economics was still in its infancy. Although some schools of thought were emerging, there were no recognized ways of understanding economic forces within society. In 2005 the economist Alan Greenspan,* former chairman of the US Federal Reserve* (the central bank of the United States), said, "For most of recorded history, people appear to have acquiesced in, and in some ways embraced, a society that was static and predictable … Smith lived at a time when market forces were beginning to erode the rigidities of the remaining feudal* and medieval practices and the mercantilism that followed them."

Greenspan points out that the ideas of the Reformation* (the break from Roman Catholicism* that saw the founding of the Protestant* Church) gained widespread support in Europe during the sixteenth century, undermining the belief that kings held a divine right to rule. Instead people began to advocate a vision of society based on individual freedom.[1]

❝ He was as great an economist as has ever lived. ❞
George J. Stigler,* "The Successes and Failures of Professor Smith"

This massive shift in social attitudes had economic repercussions. It contributed to the emergence of new economic enterprise centered around individual self-interest. This made the socioeconomic situation more complex; yet, inexplicably, the market remained stable. As Alan Greenspan wrote: "It was left to Adam Smith to identify the more general set of principles that brought conceptual clarity to the seeming chaos of market transactions."[2]

Overview of the Field

In the eighteenth century a number of thinkers sought to explain the new economic complexities that had resulted from social change in Europe. Perhaps the earliest school of systematic thought was that of the French physiocrats. Physiocracy is an economic theory that argues that a nation's wealth stems from its agricultural wealth. The physiocrats held an "agrarianist"* philosophy, viewing rural society as having an innately higher value than urban society. In the middle of the eighteenth century this group attempted to develop simple principles to explain an economic paradox. Why was it that increasing complexities in the market, such as an ever-growing volume of trade, were occurring in conjunction with a strong level of stability? In other words, how was it that supply was meeting demand?

The physiocrats concluded that economies are governed by, as Alan Greenspan later put it, "a calculable regularity—that is, natural law."[3] But, as Greenspan also wrote: "The Physiocrats' influence, however, waned rapidly along with the influence of other political economists as evidence grew that their models were, at best, incomplete."[4] Adam Smith took up the baton from these thinkers. He sought to elaborate a new and more comprehensive way of explaining how the free-market economy functions. With the publication of *The Wealth of Nations,* the first modern school of economic thought began. Smith was the founder of classical economics,* the theory that market forces will lead the economy to equilibrium. Classical economics argues that this is achieved through the price mechanism,* which creates an efficient allocation of all available resources.

Academic Influences

There were two main influences on Smith's early academic life: the Scottish Irish philosopher Francis Hutcheson,* one of his first teachers, and the Scottish philosopher David Hume.* Hutcheson was one of the most respected and well-known lecturers in Glasgow, pushing his students both to study philosophy and to incorporate it into their daily lives. So powerful was his charisma that many, including Smith, referred to him as "the never to be forgotten Hutcheson." The only other person whom Smith referred to in this way was David Hume.[5]

Smith finally met Hume in 1750 and the two formed a close bond. Although Hume was over 10 years older than Smith they had closer personal and intellectual links than perhaps any other senior figures of the Scottish Enlightenment.[6]

Another key influence on Smith was François Quesnay,* a leading figure amongst the French physiocrats. Both men rejected mercantilism, the dominant economic approach of the age. Mercantilists opposed free trade and argued that governments should accumulate resources and control the economy. The physiocrats argued for a laissez-faire* approach to the economy—that is, they believed the government should leave participants in the economic sphere to their own devices.[7]

The physiocrats' ideas had been influenced by the destructive economic policies of the French monarchy. French kings had spent vast sums to fund wars and pursue other supposedly unproductive endeavors. The physiocrats argued that the Church and nobility were parasites on the economy. Only agriculture generated wealth. This distinction between productive and unproductive labor would have a profound influence on Smith's work. Referring to "political economy,"* a term used to designate the study of the functioning of a state's economy, his conclusion was that the physiocrats had elaborated "the nearest approximation to the truth that has yet been published on the subject of political economy."[8]

NOTES

1   Alan Greenspan, "Remarks by Chairman Alan Greenspan: Adam Smith," The Federal Reserve Board, February 6, 2005, accessed October 16, 2015, http:/www.federalreserve.gov/boarddocs/speeches/2005/20050206/default.htm

2   Greenspan, "Adam Smith."

3   Greenspan, "Adam Smith."

4   Greenspan, "Adam Smith."

5   W. R. Scott, "The Never to Be Forgotten Hutcheson: Excerpts from W. R. Scott," *Econ Journal Watch* 8, no.1 (Jan 2011): 96–109.

6   Donald Winch, "Smith, Adam," *Dictionary of National Biography* (Oxford: Oxford University Press, 2004).

7   Todd Buchholz, *New Ideas from Dead Economists: An Introduction to Modern Economic Thought* (London: Penguin Books, 1999), 17.

8   Adam Smith, *An Inquiry into the Nature and Causes of the Wealth of Nations: Books I, II, III, IV and V* (New York: Metalibri Digital Edition, 2007), 526. Accessed October 16, 2015. http:/www.ibiblio.org/ml/libri/s/SmithA_WealthNations_p.pdf

MODULE 3
THE PROBLEM

KEY POINTS

- Adam Smith asks: What is the source of a nation's wealth?
- Smith also looks at the role the government should play when it comes to the economy.
- The study of economics remains divided between those who argue for greater government interference in the economy and those who argue for a free market.

Core Question

The core question in Adam Smith's *The Wealth of Nations* is: what is the source of the wealth of nations? To explore this he also addresses two key sub-questions:

- What are the dynamics that underpin economic life?
- What is the role of government in managing the economy?

Smith's work addresses the economic assumptions of his age. The dominant economic ideology of the time was mercantilism,* according to which the state should control the economy—as such, it rejected free trade. Supporters of the theory argued that a nation's wealth should be measured in terms of the amount of precious metal (gold and silver) that it possessed. As this wealth served to buttress the government, the government needed to retain the nation's stores of it and, if possible, accumulate more from other nations. This could be done by exporting as much as possible, and importing as little as possible. Smith was highly critical of mercantilism and purposely set out to challenge the intellectual basis for those who advocated greater state control of the economy.

❝ I have never known much good done by those
who affected to trade for the public good. It is
an affectation, indeed, not very common among
merchants, and very few words need be employed in
dissuading them from it. ❞

Adam Smith, *The Wealth of Nations*

In his opposition to mercantilism, Smith was preceded by the
French physiocrats,* who advocated less state control over the
economy. Smith had great respect for their ideas.

The Participants

The physiocrats and, notably, the mercantilists who had dominated
European economic thought since the sixteenth century, were the key
participants in the economic debate of the mid-eighteenth century.
Mercantilist theory led to ever-increasing levels of state involvement
in the economy; import tariffs were increased to keep foreign goods
out, inefficient industries were supported to keep exports high, and
armies and navies were used to conquer new markets by force.

The physiocrats rejected this approach to wealth creation, arguing
instead for less government interference in the economy. They
dismissed the idea that gold and silver represented the wealth of the
nation. For the physiocrats, a nation has only one source of genuine
wealth: its land. All the value in an economic system comes from
agricultural output and the products of the earth. They refused to
accept that there is value in urban life and industrialization, seeing this
simply as parasitic activity. They sought to roll back the level of state
involvement in the economy, instead arguing for a return to a situation
where trade and agricultural outputs reigned supreme.[1]

The Contemporary Debate

For Smith, the ideas of the physiocrats represented the beginnings of an economic framework for his era. He sought to further their work, giving it intellectual coherence. The Nobel prize-winning American economist George Stigler* argues that Smith's support of the physiocrats, and his attack on mercantilism, was based on the view that "unfettered individual choice in public policy was the efficiency property of competition: the manufacturer or farmer or laborer or shipper who was seeking to maximize his own income would in the very process be putting resources where they were most productive to the nation."[2] In other words, freeing up individuals to act in their own interests would result in the most productive use of a nation's resources.

Smith's work led to the rise of a school of thought known as classical economics.* At the heart of classical economics is the assumption that governments should have a relatively minimal role in economic management. The government's role should be confined to issues such as overseeing the enforcement of contracts and the protection of territory. Some of the leading proponents of classical economics were the British political economists David Ricardo* (1772–1823) and John Stuart Mill* (1806–73).

As George Stigler wrote of Smith's ideas: "From 1776 to today, the effect of this powerful attack, reinforced by the theoretical advances of Ricardo, Mill, and others, established a tradition of free international trade which even the most confirmed of economist interventionists seldom feel equal to attacking frontally."[3]

NOTES

1   Phillippe Steiner, "Physiocracy and French Pre-Classical Political Economy," in *A Companion to the History of Economic Thought*, eds. Biddle et al (Blackwell Publishing, 2003).

2   George J. Stigler, "The Successes and Failures of Professor Smith," *Journal of Political Economy*, 84 no. 6 (1976): 1201.

3   Stigler, "The Successes and Failures of Professor Smith," 1203.

MODULE 4
THE AUTHOR'S CONTRIBUTION

KEY POINTS

- Adam Smith wanted to change the prevailing attitude toward economic activity.
- *The Wealth of Nations* is divided into five books. Each book has its own theme, issue, and aim.
- Smith argues that excessive government interference in the economy will hinder wealth creation.

Author's Aims

Adam Smith's aims are very clear in *The Wealth of Nations*. As the full title of the book suggests, he wants to examine and explain "the nature and causes of the wealth of nations"—why some nations are wealthier than others, and what causes changes in a nation's wealth. He started writing the book in 1766, a decade before it was actually published. His chief aim was, perhaps, to challenge mercantilist* economics and policy-making in Britain and Europe.

Mercantilism had been the dominant economic theory in Europe since the sixteenth century. It argued for strong government control and regulation of the economy, which, it was believed, would increase national power. Mercantilism helped to support a political philosophy that justified monarchical rule—the complete and unchecked authority wielded by the hereditary head of state. It has since been contended that such absolutist* forms of government, together with mercantilism, promoted a tendency towards imperialist* ventures by prompting the pursuit of new lands and markets overseas (and the expensive wars it took to achieve these goals).[1]

> **❝ The short list of intellectuals who have materially advanced the betterment of civilization unquestionably includes Adam Smith. He is a towering contributor to the development of the modern world. ❞**
>
> Alan Greenspan,* "Adam Smith"

Notions of absolute monarchy were challenged during the period of European cultural and intellectual history known as the Enlightenment.* In *The Wealth of Nations*, Smith added his voice to those who opposed this political, social, and economic framework. He sought to provide a new intellectual framework for thinking about economic and political life.

Approach

The Wealth of Nations is divided into five books. Each has its own theme, issue and aim:

- Book 1 deals with the question of what causes economic productivity to increase; in particular Smith looks at how the division of labor can increase productivity.[2]
- Book 2 is a study of capital: how does a society accumulate wealth, and how is labor used to make that wealth productive?[3]
- In book 3 Smith switches to questions of government policy, pointing out that different nations use their resources and workforce in very different ways. For example, the "policy of some nations has given extraordinary encouragement to the industry of the country; that of others to the industry of towns." Further: "Since the downfall of the Roman empire, the policy of Europe has been more favourable to arts, manufactures, and commerce … than to agriculture." He says that the core question for the third book is to explain the "circumstances which seem to have introduced and established this policy."[4]

- Smith highlights that the policies of Europe, favoring industry over agriculture, were "first introduced by the private interests and prejudices of particular orders of men, without any regard to … the general welfare of the society." In book 4 he seeks "to explain … those different theories, and the principle effects which they have produced in different ages and nations."[5]
- In book 5, Smith moves on from an examination of "what has consisted the revenue of the great body of the people" to deal with the "revenue of the sovereign, or commonwealth." He looks at the necessary expenses of the sovereign or commonwealth and the best methods of collecting taxes. Finally, he asks why "almost all modern governments … mortgage some part of this revenue, or contract debts, and what have been the effects of those debts upon the real wealth, the annual produce of the land and labour of the society."[6]

Contribution in Context

One of Adam Smith's aims in *The Wealth of Nations* was to overthrow the intellectual justification for the mercantilist school of thought, then dominant in European political circles. This held that the wealth of nations was determined by their store of gold and silver. There were two resulting policy implications:

- The role of the state was to protect industries and other sectors, by force if necessary.
- The state needed to prevent the outflow of gold and silver.

The perception this created was that international trade was a zero-sum game:* In other words, any economic gain made by one nation caused a direct, corresponding loss to another. The fear of losing gold and silver meant that trade was avoided.

Smith sought to change this mindset. He highlighted the idea that trade can make all participants better off. At the heart of his argument is the idea that behind the apparent chaos of the market and international trade, there lies a series of economic forces that keep society in balance and contribute to the creation of new wealth. As a result, trade can increase the well-being of a society. In his book, Smith argues that when individuals behave in a way that is conducive to their own self-interest, the outcome is that they benefit, and that society more broadly also benefits. The implication is that by hindering trade, government interference impedes both the creation of wealth and an increase in social well-being.

NOTES

1   R. Nester, *The Great Frontier War: Britain, France, and the Imperial Struggle for North America, 1607–1755* (Westport, Conn: Praeger, 2000).

2   Adam Smith, *An Inquiry into the Nature and Causes of the Wealth of Nations: Books I, II, III, IV and V* (New York: Metalibri Digital Edition, 2007), 4.

3   Smith, *The Wealth of Nations*, 5.

4   Smith, *The Wealth of Nations*, 5.

5   Smith, *The Wealth of Nations*, 5.

6   Smith, *The Wealth of Nations*, 5.

SECTION 2
IDEAS

MAIN IDEAS

KEY POINTS

- Smith's key idea in *The Wealth of Nations* is that self-interested individuals operating within a competitive marketplace can produce economic prosperity.

- Smith's ideas were underpinned by a strong liberal* belief in the value of individual freedom and autonomy.

- *The Wealth of Nations* was written in an accessible and straightforward style.

Key Themes

The key idea in Adam Smith's book *The Wealth of Nations* is that broader economic prosperity is prompted by people working to further their own interests. For this to happen, the work done has to be rational (that is, it has to be of value) and it has to take place within a competitive marketplace. When these conditions are met, it is as though an "invisible hand"* is governing economic activity, making markets effective and stable.

As Smith wrote: "It is not from the benevolence of the butcher, the brewer, or the baker, that we expect our dinner, but from their regard to their own interest."[1] In other words, individuals are not productive out of a sense of charity. They produce for their own well-being. Their selfish desires result in an increase in economic output, which in turn leads to an increase in available goods in society, such as food. This, therefore, increases the well-being of society as a whole. While many people would view selfishness as a vice, for Smith, in a market economy, selfishness produces social benefits.

❝ By preferring the support of domestic to that of foreign industry, [the individual] intends only his own security; and by directing that industry in such a manner as its produce may be of the greatest value, he intends only his own gain, and he is in this, as in many other cases, led by an invisible hand to promote an end which was no part of his intention. ❞

Adam Smith, *The Wealth of Nations*

One of the implications of these arguments is that the government's role within the economy should be to enable individual enterprise. In 2005 the American economist Alan Greenspan* highlighted one way in which this was done. He said that as laws were passed to protect individual rights and individual property, an increase in productivity, innovation, and trade soon followed. "A whole new system of enterprise began to develop, which, though it seemed bewildering in its complexity and consequences, appeared nonetheless to possess a degree of stability as if guided by an 'invisible hand.'"[2]

Exploring the Ideas

Freedom and competition are both fundamental aspects of Smith's economic philosophy. Greenspan notes that "[Smith] concluded that the competitive force unleashed by individuals in pursuit of their rational self-interest induces each person to do better. Such competitive interaction, by encouraging specialization and division of labor, increases economic growth."[3]

Smith's belief in the value of individual freedom and autonomy grew from his Enlightenment* philosophy of liberalism. Liberals believed in the improvement of the individual through learning and societal progress. The economic potential of the free market, Smith argued, would come to fruition if "Every man, as long as he does not violate the laws of justice, is left perfectly free to pursue his own interest his own way, and to bring both his industry and capital into competition with those of any other man, or order of men."[4]

Smith's free-market ideas called for individuals to be free to pursue their own perceived economic self-interest, unhampered by government. If the government makes too many economic decisions—who should produce what and in what quantities; who should trade with whom; who should learn what—then this will squeeze out freedom and economic well-being. For Smith, individuals should be left to pursue their own ends, even if those ends are technically selfish; this is the way to make society richer, economically productive, and politically stable.

Language and Expression

The Wealth of Nations is an extremely accessible text. As the English historian Edward Gibbon* wrote at the time of publication:"What an excellent work is that with which our common friend Mr. Adam Smith has enriched the public! An extensive science in a single book, and the most profound ideas expressed in the most perspicuous language."[5] Smith's writing style was so clear that some thought it was too easy. Smith's supporters said the book was unfairly "ridiculed for its simplicity."[6]

As refreshingly jargon-free as Smith's writing style may be, *The Wealth of Nations* is an extremely long text; there are lengthy digressions, and scholars warn of the hidden complexity of the work. Many argue that the text can be interpreted in various ways due to ambiguities in its arguments; more, extracts from the book have been used out of context to suggest broad pronouncements on Smith's part that he was not making. As the American academic Samuel Fleischacker writes: "Scholars have persistently misread the *Wealth of Nations*, and I'd like to show right off why it is easy to do that. [The book] tends to appear, in both scholarly and popular literature, by way of striking snippets.

One can properly grasp its teachings, however, only by engaging in the painstaking exercise of reading the long, elaborate arguments from which the snippets get snipped."[7]

In other words, to read Smith correctly it is vital to understand some very lengthy and complex arguments. When people look to Smith for short and quickly summarized ideas and quotes, they can lose the thread of his wider point. As a result they can mistakenly find justification for ideas that the book does not offer.

NOTES

1   Adam Smith, *An Inquiry into the Nature and Causes of the Wealth of Nations: Books I, II, III, IV and V* (New York: Metalibri Digital Edition, 2007), 16.

2   Alan Greenspan, "Remarks by Chairman Alan Greenspan: Adam Smith," The Federal Reserve Board, February 6, 2005, accessed October 16, 2015, http://www.federalreserve.gov/boarddocs/speeches/2005/20050206/default.htm

3   Greenspan, "Adam Smith."

4   Smith, *The Wealth of Nations*, 533.

5   John Rae, *Life of Adam Smith* (London: Macmillan & Co., 1895), 287.

6   Rae, *Life of Adam Smith*, 290.

7   Samuel Fleischacker, *On Adam Smith's "Wealth of Nations": A Philosophical Companion* (Princeton: Princeton University Press, 2004), 3.

MODULE 6
SECONDARY IDEAS

KEY POINTS

- *The Wealth of Nations* addresses ideas about individual liberty, economic freedom, and the efficiency of the free market.

- These ideas, also known as "laissez-faire"* or ("allow to do" or "let it be") originated with the French physiocrats,* economic thinkers of the eighteenth century who argued that national wealth is derived from agricultural wealth.

- New scholarship is looking at Smith's arguments about the role of the state in promoting equality and providing public works.

Other Ideas

In his book *The Wealth of Nations*, Adam Smith writes extensively about individual liberty, economic freedom, and the efficiency of the free market. Smith also makes a case against strong government intervention in, or control over, the economy, stating, "The sovereign [government] is completely discharged from a duty, in the attempting to perform which no human wisdom or knowledge could ever be sufficient; the duty of superintending the industry of private people, and of directing it towards the employments most suitable to the interest of society."[1]

In other words, to seek to direct economic life is impossible and the ruler is under no obligation to attempt this impossible task. Smith argues that rulers should never have attempted to do this in the first place. He calls it "the highest impertinence and presumption … in kings and ministers, to pretend to watch over the economy of private

❝ Let [kings and ministers] look well after their own expense, and they may safely trust private people with theirs. If their own extravagance does not ruin the state, that of their subjects never will. ❞

Adam Smith, *The Wealth of Nations*

people, and to restrain their expense … They are themselves always, and without any exception, the greatest spendthrifts in the society."[2]

Smith's ideas about lifting artificial, state-controlled restrictions on trade are known as "laissez-faire" ideas. They originated with the French physiocrats, a group of thinkers who had a tremendous influence on him.

Exploring the Ideas

The popular story is that the phrase "laissez-faire" ("let it be") was first heard in 1681, when the French minister for finance, Jean-Baptiste Colbert,* a man whose mercantilist* approach was reflected in his belief in state control of the economy, met a group of French business leaders. When Colbert asked the merchants how the government could boost commerce and thereby increase the wealth and power of the French state, the recorded response highlighted the emerging belief in government non-interference: "Let it be, that should be the motto of all public powers, since the world was civilized … That we cannot grow except by lowering our neighbors is a detestable notion! Only malice and malignity of heart is satisfied with such a principle and our (national) interest is opposed to it. Let it be, for heaven's sake! Let it be!"[3]

In *The Wealth of Nations* Smith illustrates (what he argues is) the absurdity of attempting to direct economic life by referring to laws that restrict economic freedom; for him, while the authorities claim that these laws protect the greater good of society, their real effect is to lessen economic well-being:"The exclusive privileges of corporations, statutes of apprenticeship, and all those laws which restrain, in particular employments, the competition to a smaller number than might otherwise go into them, have the same tendency, though in a less degree."[4]

By reducing competition, these laws restrict productivity; indeed, Smith argues that these laws allow corporations to become "enlarged monopolies"* that are frequently able to keep the market price of particular commodities unnaturally high. As a consequence, wages and profits remain far higher than they would be without these laws.[5] This may benefit the corporations, but it does not benefit society as a whole.

Overlooked

Although most scholars have focused on Smith's ideas about the "free market,"* in recent years, scholars have started to look at what he had to say about the role of the state in promoting equality and providing public works. Smith argues that the government has three main duties: "According to the system of natural liberty, the sovereign has only three duties to attend to: ... first, the duty of protecting the society from violence and invasion from other independent societies; secondly, the duty of protecting, as far as possible, every member of the society from the injustice or oppression of every other member of it, or the duty of establishing an exact administration of justice; and, thirdly, the duty of erecting and maintaining certain public works and certain public institutions which it can never be for the interest of any individual, or small number of individuals, to erect and maintain."[6]

Smith also acknowledges that there are moral and practical problems with the capitalist* economy, highlighting, for example, the problems of landlords, whose role is "passive" rather than "productive." Instead of creating wealth, they simply own and observe parts of the economic process. Smith says that this makes them "indolent and inept, and so they tend to be unable to even look after their own economic interests."[7] These problems then extend to the broader economy. Smith argues that landlords should be in favor of policies that contribute to wealth increase. Increased productivity leads to increased food, which supports population growth. Growth increases the need for food, which tends towards greater productivity (getting more from the land to meet the increased demand). This should increase rents, which is economically beneficial to landlords. But Smith argues that landlords are opposed to these pro-growth policies on account of their own "indolent-induced ignorance and intellectual flabbiness."[8]

NOTES

1   Adam Smith, *An Inquiry into the Nature and Causes of the Wealth of Nations: Books I, II, III, IV and V* (New York: Metalibri Digital Edition, 2007), 533.

2   Smith, *The Wealth of Nations*, 346.

3   John Maynard Keynes, *The End of Laissez-Faire* (New York: Prometheus Books, 2004).

4   Smith, *The Wealth of Nations*, 52.

5   Smith, *The Wealth of Nations*, 52.

6   Smith, *The Wealth of Nations*, 534.

7   Spencer J. Pack, *Capitalism as a Moral System: Adam Smith's Critique of the Free Market Economy* (Aldershot: Edward Elgar, 2010).

8   Pack, *Capitalism as a Moral System*.

MODULE 7
ACHIEVEMENT

KEY POINTS

- *The Wealth of Nations* revolutionized economic and political thought.

- The book was an instant success. Its first edition sold out within six months.

- Some of Smith's ideas—his use of the labor theory of value,* for example, according to which the value of goods and services is determined by the labor required to produce them—are no longer used.

Assessing the Argument

Adam Smith's book *The Wealth of Nations* revolutionized economic and political thought. One of the most important works in the history of ideas, it led to Smith's reputation as the father of modern economics. Before Smith, people had produced many economic theories; ancient Greek and Roman, South Asian, Chinese, Persian, and Arab civilizations all made contributions to economic theory according to their own traditions, while the thirteenth-century religious thinker and philosopher Thomas Aquinas* has been described as the person who came the closest to establishing a "scientific economics" before Smith.[1]

It was not until the emergence of mercantilism* in the sixteenth century, however, that a coherent school of economic thought became ingrained in government policy-making. In the eighteenth century, the French physiocrats* challenged mercantilist ideas about state control of the economy, which they believed contrary to the functioning of a healthy market—but they failed to develop a clear

❝ The most important substantive proposition in all of economics. **❞**

George Stigler,* "The Successes and Failures of Professor Smith"

and coherent framework for understanding how order could exist within an apparently chaotic economic system.

Smith, in contrast, did produce a coherent argument and framework regarding how the market economy* functions, and this allowed scientific enquiry into economic life. Various schools of thought grew from his work. The first of these was the classical* school of economics, which, by the late nineteenth century, had developed into the neoclassical* school (an approach to economic theory founded on three assumptions—that people are rational and have preferences based on value; that people maximize their own well-being while firms maximize profits; and that people have full and relevant information on which to act).

While the discipline splintered into other subsections during the twentieth century, all can be traced back to Smith's central arguments about the free market and the invisible hand.*

Achievement in Context

The Wealth of Nations was an instant success. Its first edition sold out within six months[2] and its influence was immediately apparent among political figures and economic thinkers.

In nineteenth-century England, Smith's ideas were the foundation for influential schools of thought in political economy. For example, the English statesman Richard Cobden*(1804–65) founded the Manchester School,* which rejected protectionism* (taxing foreign imports to protect the domestic economy); this school argued against the Corn Laws* in England—laws aimed at protecting English agriculture from overseas competition—and advocated free trade. In contrast, other thinkers rejected the free-trade ideology of the Manchester School and highlighted Smith's proposal for an imperial federation.*

The Wealth of Nations figured prominently in both sides' arguments. As one commentator writes, "On the one hand, Adam Smith's late nineteenth- and early twentieth-century Cobdenite adherents used his theories to argue for gradual imperial devolution and empire 'on the cheap.' On the other hand, various proponents of imperial federation throughout the British world sought to use Smith's theories to overturn the predominant Cobdenite hands-off imperial approach and instead, with a firm grip, bring the empire closer than ever before."[3]

In other words, Smith's arguments were used by those arguing for more control over the empire and by those arguing for greater freedom from government control.

Limitations

Despite the breadth of Smith's work, *The Wealth of Nations* has limitations. Some aspects of its framework for economic analysis have fallen out of favor. For example, the classical economists who followed Smith could not agree on what he meant by the "labor theory of value." This is an economic theory that values goods or services in terms of the amount of labor that is needed to produce them. Smith's own views are ambiguous. Some classical economists believe that he provides a loose justification for the theory. Neoclassical economists reject this. They argue that the value of a good is determined by what someone will give up in order to obtain it.[4]

This is not the only idea in *The Wealth of Nations* that is open to different interpretations. Some argue that the book contains implicit support for a minimum wage.[5] Others say it makes a clear statement against wage regulation: "The price of labour, it must be observed, cannot be ascertained very accurately anywhere, different prices being often paid at the same place and for the same sort of labour, not only according to the different abilities of the workmen, but according to the easiness or hardness of the masters. Where wages are not regulated by law, all that we can pretend to determine is what are the most usual; and experience seems to show that law can never regulate them properly, though it has often pretended to do so."[6]

Later economists were also highly critical of Smith's idea of the "invisible hand." This remains a divisive notion among academics and policymakers; many feel it is based on blind faith in economic outcomes, and that it creates an approach to economics that is overly deferential to existing moneyed interests.

NOTES

1   Joseph A Schumpeter, *History of Economic Analysis*, (New York: Oxford University Press, 1954), 97–115.

2   Todd Buchholz, *New Ideas from Dead Economists: An Introduction to Modern Economic Thought* (London: Penguin Books, 1999), 19.

3   Marc-William Palen, "Adam Smith as Advocate of Empire, c. 1870–1932," *Historical Journal* 57, no. 1 (2014): 179–98.

4   Stanley W. Jevons, *The Theory of Political Economy*, 2nd edition (London: Macmillan, 1879), xiv.

5   Christopher Martin, "Adam Smith and Liberal Economics: Reading the Minimum Wage Debate of 1795–96," *Econ Journal Watch* 8, no. 2 (2011): 110–25.

6   Adam Smith, *An Inquiry into the Nature and Causes of the Wealth of Nations: Books I, II, III, IV and V* (New York: Metalibri Digital Edition, 2007), 65.

MODULE 8
PLACE IN THE AUTHOR'S WORK

KEY POINTS

- *The Wealth of Nations* is Smith's second main work. His first was *The Theory of Moral Sentiments*, which was published in 1759.

- *The Wealth of Nations* is seen, increasingly, as a continuation of *The Theory of Moral Sentiments*.

- The significance of Smith's work lies in its originality and its breadth.

Positioning

The Wealth of Nations is Adam Smith's second main work. The first was *The Theory of Moral Sentiments*, which he published in 1759.[1] This was a work of moral philosophy* discussing the genesis of moral thinking and based on lectures Smith gave in Glasgow—and Smith himself is believed to have regarded it as his greatest work. Within it he concludes that morality arises from the interaction of individuals in society. In other words, despite humankind's natural tendency towards self-interested behavior, observing other people helps us to become aware of our own behavior. This "theory of sympathy" leads to greater morality within society.[2]

The ideas in *The Theory of Moral Sentiments* predict many of those explored in *The Wealth of Nations*. Over the years Smith gradually shifted the emphasis in his work away from the study of morality toward the study of economics and law.[3] He began to challenge the ideas underpinning mercantilism* and started to argue that increases in national wealth actually derive from labor,[4] an early rejection of mercantilism that set the stage for *The Wealth of Nations*.

❝ The administration of the great system of the universe ... the care of the universal happiness of all rational and sensible beings, is the business of God and not of man. To man is allotted a much humbler department, but one much more suitable to the weakness of his powers, and to the narrowness of his comprehension: the care of his own happiness, of that of his family, his friends, his country ... But though we are ... endowed with a very strong desire of those ends, it has been entrusted to the slow and uncertain determinations of our reason to find out the proper means of bringing them about. ❞

Adam Smith, *The Theory of Moral Sentiments*

Integration

Initially, the scholarly debate of Smith's works highlighted a tension between the ideas outlined in *The Theory of Moral Sentiments* and those contained in *The Wealth of Nations*. While Smith's first book highlights individual morality, his second was viewed as advocating self-interest; many claimed that it advocated self-interest above all else.[5] More recently, however, scholars have highlighted the similarity between Smith's books.[6] For example, his "theory of sympathy," introduced in *The Theory of Moral Sentiments*, argues that the greater good can be pursued, indirectly, through rational, self-interested behavior. As several scholars have pointed out, the two works highlight different aspects of human nature operating under different circumstances. For example, the American economists Robert Ekelund and Robert Hebert write that "in [*The Theory of Moral Sentiments*], sympathy is the moral faculty that holds self-interest in check, whereas in [*The Wealth of Nations*], competition is the economic faculty that restrains self-interest."[7]

This tendency to view *The Theory of Moral Sentiments* and *The Wealth of Nations* as a coherent body of work that should be read together has been developing since the 1970s. It was driven, in part, by a resurgence of interest in Smith's work following the bicentenary of *The Wealth of Nations* in 1976.

Significance

The significance of Smith's work lies in its originality and its breadth. Smith synthesized ideas that had emerged under the French physiocrats,* merged them with the economic and political realities of the period, and drafted them into a coherent framework for economic thought. *The Wealth of Nations* prompted generations of thinkers to elaborate on, and later challenge, Smith's central insights. The most influential economists of the twentieth century all formulated their ideas in reference to Smith. The British economist John Maynard Keynes,* for example, wrote in direct opposition to the ideas of Smith; Keynesian* economics rejects the idea that the free-market economy* tends towards a "natural" balance, or equilibrium. Instead he claims that Smith and later classical* or neoclassical* economists misunderstood the determinants of employment, and therefore the causes of economic instability.

In turn, later scholars used Smith's ideas to challenge the ideas of Keynes. The Austrian British economist Friedrich Von Hayek* and the American economist Milton Friedman* reiterate the central messages of *The Wealth of Nations*.[8] They point to the inability of the government to bring order to the chaos of the free market. Their argument is that Smith's "invisible hand,"* a force that guides supply and demand, should be trusted to bring order to the seeming economic chaos. Friedman argues that government intervention in the economy brings unintended consequences. In his 1968 paper "The Role of Monetary Policy," Friedman highlights that government efforts to manage the level of unemployment had no long-term impact. Instead, he claims, the effect was merely to drive up the overall level of prices.[9]

NOTES

1   Adam Smith, *The Theory of Moral Sentiments*, edited by Knud Haakonssen (Cambridge: Cambridge University Press, 2002).

2   Smith, *The Theory of Moral Sentiments*.

3   James Buchan, *The Authentic Adam Smith: His Life and Ideas* (New York: W. W. Norton & Company, 2006), 67.

4   Todd Buchholz, *New Ideas from Dead Economists: An Introduction to Modern Economic Thought* (London: Penguin Books, 1999), 15.

5   Jacob Viner, in *Essays on the Intellectual History of Economics*, ed. Douglas A. Irwin (Princeton, NJ: Princeton University Press, 1991), 250.

6   Lionel Robbins, *A History of Economic Thought*, (Princeton, NJ: Princeton University Press, 1998).

7   R. Ekelund & R. Hebert, *A History of Economic Theory and Method*, 5th edition (Long Grove, IL: Waveland Press, 2007), 105.

8   F. A. Hayek, *The Road to Serfdom* (Chicago, IL: University of Chicago Press, 1994); Milton Friedman and Rose D. Friedman, *Capitalism and Freedom*, 40th ed. (Chicago, IL: University of Chicago Press, 2002).

9   Milton Friedman, "The Role of Monetary Policy," *American Economic Review* 58 (1968): 1–17.

SECTION 3
IMPACT

MODULE 9
THE FIRST RESPONSES

KEY POINTS

- Early critics of Smith's work focused on what they saw as the agrarian*-centric nature of his analysis (that is, its focus on the links between wealth and agriculture).

- The first systematic challenge to Smith's free-market* ideas was posed by the British economist John Maynard Keynes* in the twentieth century.

- Classical economics* enjoyed a resurgence in the later part of the twentieth century.

Criticism

The ideas in Adam Smith's book *The Wealth of Nations* have been debated for over two centuries. Early critics rejected Smith's agrarian-focused arguments (that is, the idea that wealth is based on agriculture and the land). For example, Alexander Hamilton,* the first finance minister of the young United States, took many of Smith's assertions apart. In his *Report on Manufactures*, presented to the US Congress in 1791, Hamilton rejected the free-trade arguments outlined in *The Wealth of Nations*. He argued that the new US republic required highly protectionist* policies to encourage economic development and cement its independence from Britain.[1] Others, among them the third president of the United States, Thomas Jefferson,* favored agrarian policies and gave positive coverage of Smith's work.[2]

Smith's ideas were also being discussed amongst British politicians. In 1783 the prominent statesman Charles James Fox spoke in Parliament, saying, "There was a maxim laid down in an excellent book upon the *Wealth of Nations* which had been ridiculed for its

> ❝[On] the subjects of money & commerce, Smith's
> *Wealth of Nations* is the best book to be read, unless
> Say's *Political Economy* can be had, which treats the same
> subject on the same principles, but in a shorter compass
> & more lucid manner.❞
>
> Thomas Jefferson,* *Writings*

simplicity, but which was indisputable as to its truth. In that book it was stated that the only way to become rich was to manage matters so as to make one's income exceed one's expenses. This maxim applied equally to an individual and to a nation. The proper line of conduct therefore was by a well-directed economy to retrench every current expense, and to make as large a saving during the peace as possible."[3]

The Wealth of Nations contributed to the rapid decline in mercantilist* thinking at the end of the eighteenth century. The onset of the Industrial Revolution* in Britain resulted in an economic system that favored Smith's ideas. These were cemented by the emergence of the British Empire, which promoted liberal,* free-trade models emphasizing economic freedom and a minimum of governmental interference around the world, and used its naval force to sustain global trade routes.[4]

Responses

A systematic intellectual critique of free-market economics did not emerge until the twentieth century. But in 1936 the field of economics was rocked by an intellectual earthquake: the "Keynesian* revolution."[5] In his book *The General Theory of Employment, Interest and Money*, the British economist John Maynard Keynes outlined a set of ideas that challenged Smith. The work divided economists into two main camps. On the one side were liberals and socialists* (those, very roughly, who believe that industry should be held in public hands, and that profits should be invested in state institutions). These groups favored the Keynesian notion that market economies* tend to be inherently unstable and therefore require more active government intervention. On the other side were classical economists of the Smithian tradition who rejected Keynes's ideas, believing in the effectiveness of market economies and pointing to the problems of government intervention.

In the 1950s and 1960s Keynesianism—economic policy based on the theories proposed by Keynes—reached its peak. US President Richard Nixon*—a staunch economic conservative and anti-communist*—proved this point in 1971, saying, "I am now a Keynesian."[6] But during the 1970s and 1980s economists such as Milton Friedman* and Friedrich von Hayek* led a successful counterrevolution against Keynesian ideas.

Hayek had published a work that directly challenged Keynes as early as 1944.[7] In *The Road to Serfdom* he argued that no individual (or group of individuals) had enough information to govern entire economic processes, let alone the economy as a whole. In the 1960s, Hayek's work was furthered by Milton Friedman. Friedman challenged many of the policy-making practices of the post-World War II* era and argued for the need for a return to free-market economics. His school of thought became known as monetarism.*[8]

Conflict and Consensus

After the publication of Keynes' *The General Theory* in 1936, Keynesian economics commanded widespread adherence among economists. Those arguing for a more classical, "free-market," understanding of economics (such as Milton Friedman) were relegated to the margins of the discipline. Governments pursued policies that actively aimed at managing the economy. But in 1968 Friedman published the paper "The Role of Monetary Policy." This sought to address the broader debate between Keynesian economists and those arguing for a less interventionist government role in the economy.

Friedman wanted to discuss the real effects of a proactive monetary policy*—that is, the governmental policy of working to stimulate the economy by actively adjusting both the amount of money in circulation and interest rates, rather than allowing them to be determined by the market. He argued that this approach was far less effective than Keynesian policymakers believed, and might actually have detrimental consequences for economic stability.[9] Even Friedman's critics agreed about the impact of his arguments. In 1995, the American economist James Tobin, a longstanding critic of Friedman's work, described this paper as "very likely the most influential article ever published in an economics journal." The American economist Paul Krugman* called it "one of the decisive achievements of the postwar era," while the British economic historian Robert Skidelsky argued that it is "easily the most influential paper on macroeconomics [economic functions below the scale of the nation] ever published in the postwar era."[10]

Both Hayek and Friedman directly influenced policy-making. Under British prime minister Margaret Thatcher* and American president Ronald Reagan,* Keynesian economics was forced into retreat. This was also prompted by the onset of stagflation* in the 1970s. With economic stagnation* occurring at the same time as inflation* (rising prices) more questions were raised about the efficacy of government intervention in the economy. The public mood was once again receptive to traditional Smithian free-market values.

NOTES

1   Douglas A. Irwin, "The Aftermath of Hamilton's 'Report on Manufactures,'" *The Journal of Economic History,* 64, no. 3 (2004): 800–21.

2   Thomas Jefferson, *Writings,* (The Library of America, 1984), 1176.

3   John Rae, *Life of Adam Smith* (London: Macmillan & Co., 1895), 290.

4   L. Seabrooke, *Global Standards of Market Civilization,* (London: Taylor & Francis, 2006), 192.

5   John Maynard Keynes, *The General Theory of Employment, Interest and Money* in *The Collected Writings of John Maynard Keynes, Volume VII* (London: Macmillan/St. Martin's Press, 1973).

6   Richard Nixon, quoted in Paul Krugman, "Plutocracy, Paralysis, Perplexity," *New York Times* (May 3, 2012), A29.

7   F. A. Hayek, *The Road to Serfdom* (Chicago: University of Chicago Press, 1994).

8   Milton Friedman and Rose D. Friedman, *Capitalism and Freedom,* 40th ed. (Chicago, IL: University of Chicago Press, 2002).

9   Milton Friedman, "The Role of Monetary Policy," *American Economic Review* 58 (1968): 1–17.

10 Brian Snowdon and Howard R. Vane, *Modern Macroeconomics: Its Origins, Development and Current State,* 1st ed. (Cheltenham: Edward Elgar Publishing, 2005), 175.

MODULE 10
THE EVOLVING DEBATE

KEY POINTS

- All aspects of Smith's work have been highly contested and debated.

- A variety of economic schools of thought have emerged since Smith. The main ones are the classical* school, the neoclassical* school, and the Keynesian* school.

- Smith is still referenced by contemporary economists and his ideas continue to be debated.

Uses and Problems

Adam Smith's book *The Wealth of Nations* deals with a vast number of economic concepts. Some of these have been interpreted and implemented in different ways. One key example is the idea of the "labor theory of value,"* which suggests that the value of goods or services is determined by the amount of labor needed to produce them.

Classical economists developed a number of theories that elaborated on the labor theory of value. These frequently contradicted one other. Later, neoclassical economists also contested the theory, arguing that the value of a good is determined by what someone is willing to give up to obtain it. In other words, they claimed that the value of a product cannot be determined by quantifying the value of the labor that went into producing it. This led to neoclassical economics being referred to as "marginalism."*[1] The value of a product is not a fixed, essential part of that product. It fluctuates, depending on the benefits it offers to a particular person at a particular time. So, value is defined by the margin between what something costs

❝ If the Treasury were to fill old bottles with banknotes, bury them at suitable depths in disused coalmines which are then filled up to the surface with town rubbish, and leave it to private enterprise on well-tried principles of laissez-faire to dig the notes up again ... there need be no more unemployment. ❞

John Maynard Keynes,* *The General Theory of Employment, Interest and Money*

to produce and how much it is wanted by a prospective buyer. Today, mainstream economics largely rejects the labor theory of value.[2]

Schools of Thought

The Wealth of Nations led to the formation of the classical school of economic thought, generally considered the foundation of modern economics.[3] Smith's work became the focal point for economic study. For over 150 years his ideas were the unchallenged starting point for understanding the market economy.* In 1936 the British economist John Maynard Keynes* published his systematic critique of free-market economics* and the self-correcting market. In *The General Theory of Employment, Interest and Money* Keynes developed an alternative approach to understanding the market economy. Instead of seeing it as inherently stable, Keynes argued that markets had a tendency towards instability. He pointed to the Great Depression,* the severe economic downturn that occurred during the 1930s that wreaked economic and political havoc around the world.[4]

Keynes argues that traditional economics had misunderstood the causes of full employment.* Following Smith, classical economists believed that employment was determined by the price of labor. Keynes argues that it is aggregate demand*—that is, total demand—that determines employment. A shortfall in demand could result in a downward cycle: lower demand fuels less employment and then even lower demand, resulting in prolonged underemployment. This idea challenges the basis of Smithian free-market economics: that economies are more efficient if left free of outside interference. Keynes argues that economies require government intervention in order to stabilize at times of crisis.

The onset of the most severe and prolonged depression on record—the Great Depression*—caused many to question the core assumption of classical economics. As Keynes wrote to his friend, the Irish playwright and socialist George Bernard Shaw:* "I believe myself to be writing a book on economic theory which will largely revolutionize—not I suppose, at once but in the course of the next ten years—the way the world thinks about its economic problems."[5]

In Current Scholarship

While Adam Smith and *The Wealth of Nations* generally enjoy extremely high regard among economists, both have their critics. As the Austrian American economist Joseph Schumpeter* wrote, "His very limitation made for success. Had he been more brilliant, he would not have been taken so seriously. Had he dug more deeply, had he unearthed more recondite truth, had he used more difficult and ingenious methods, he would not have been understood. But he had no such ambitions; in fact he disliked whatever went beyond plain common sense. He never moved above the heads of even the dullest readers. He led them on gently, encouraging them by trivialities and homely observations, making them feel comfortable all along."[6]

Yet, despite the criticisms, Smith is considered the father of modern economics. In the 1970s there was a resurgence of academic interest in his work that led to an increased focus on his earlier book, *The Theory of Moral Sentiments*.[7] The "rediscovery" of Smith's moral philosophy* added a new dimension to the debate. *Homo economicus* ("economic man") was not only an economic creature, he was also a moral creature.

New scholarship seeks to imbue Smith's work with modern liberal*
principles, by focusing on his apparent disdain for religious and social
hierarchies and highlighting his opposition to the British Empire.[8]
Other scholarship explores his ideas about Britain's rebellious colonies
in the Americas, which would soon claim their independence to form
the United States—Smith advocated both independence and a close
colonial system of trade. This ambiguity resulted in different thinkers
choosing the recommendations they preferred.[9]

NOTES

1 Antonietta Campos, "Marginalist Economics," *The New Palgrave: A
 Dictionary of Economics, Volume III* (1987), 320.

2 Joan Robinson, *Economic Philosophy* (Piscataway, NJ: Transaction
 Publishers, 2006), 39.

3 John J. McCusker, *Mercantilism and the Economic History of the Early
 Modern Atlantic World* (Cambridge: Cambridge University Press, 2001).

4 John Maynard Keynes, *The General Theory of Employment, Interest and
 Money* in *The Collected Writings of John Maynard Keynes, Volume VII*
 (London: Macmillan/St. Martin's Press, 1973).

5 John Cassidy, "The Demand Doctor," *New Yorker*, October 10,
 2011, accessed October 26, 2015, http://www.newyorker.com/
 magazine/2011/10/10/the-demand-doctor

6 Joseph Schumpeter, *History of Economic Analysis* (New York: Oxford
 University Press), 185.

7 Adam Smith, *The Theory of Moral Sentiments*, edited by Knud Haakonssen
 (Cambridge: Cambridge University Press, 2002).

8 David M. Levy & Sandra J. Peart, "The Secret History of the Dismal Science.
 Part I. Economics, Religion and Race in the 19th Century," *Library of
 Economics and Liberty*, January 22, 2001, accessed October 19, 2015,
 http://www.econlib.org/library/Columns/LevyPeartdismal.html

9 E. A. Benians, "Adam Smith's Project of an Empire," *Cambridge Historical
 Journal* 1 (1925): 249–83.

MODULE 11
IMPACT AND INFLUENCE TODAY

KEY POINTS

- All students of economics are expected to be very much aware of *The Wealth of Nations*.

- Adam Smith is viewed as the intellectual father of free-market economics.*

- The discipline of economics remains split between those who believe in the efficiency of the free market and those who believe that the free market is inherently unstable.

Position

Adam Smith's *The Wealth of Nations* remains a foundational text in the study of economics. Smith is widely considered to be one of the founders of economic study and his ideas are still central to all debates and discussions within the field. Any resurgence in free-market thinking is frequently accompanied by a direct increase in interest in Smith's work, as he is viewed as synonymous with free-market ideals.

The Wealth of Nations is well known outside the field of economics. In 2005 it was chosen as one of the 100 Best Scottish Books of all time.[1] Politicians and political thinkers point to Smith as an influence on their thinking; his economic standing was underlined in 2007, when the Bank of England made him the first Scotsman to feature on a British banknote.[2]

Various think tanks and institutes around the world also hold Smith's memory in high esteem. One example is the Adam Smith Institute in London, a think tank that promotes ideas and policy proposals based on Smith's free-market ideals. Another is the Cato Institute in the United States, which promotes free-market ideas through briefings, public debate, and by training policymakers.

> **66** In 1776, Smith produced one of the great
> achievements in human intellectual history: *An Inquiry
> into the Nature and Causes of the Wealth of Nations.* Most
> of Smith's free-market paradigm remains applicable to
> this day. **99**

Alan Greenspan,* "Adam Smith"

Interaction

Adam Smith's *The Wealth of Nations* is the standard-bearer for free-market economics. The book reveals the dynamics of the market economy* and provides an explanatory framework for economic outcomes. Instead of seeing the market as chaotic, Smith highlights its underlying order and its ability to produce optimal economic outcomes.

The text is still of vital use to economists, political scientists, policymakers and broader audiences. It is essential for understanding the debate between those who call for governmental intervention in a state's economic and social life and those who advocate a more minimalist governmental role.

The core idea outlined by Smith and elaborated on by later classical* economists is that market economies are self-regulating and therefore best left free of government intervention. When governments intervene in the market, they often do so for political reasons. Although they claim to be operating in the public interest, they often do exactly the opposite.

The American economist George Stigler* highlights that Smith's work contains "the most important substantive proposition in all of economics." Stigler says this is the idea that, when markets operate competitively, the owners of productive resources—land, labor, capital, and enterprise—will engage their resources in the most profitable and thereby efficient way. This is now the basis for "resource-allocation theory,"* which examines the allocation of scarce resources between various possible uses.[3]

The Continuing Debate

The way in which Smith contributed to "laissez-faire"* free-market economics, in which the economy is left free of government interference in the belief that it will regulate itself to the benefit of its participants, is still debated. Many point to Smith's fundamental role in shaping a belief in free markets and minimal government interference. Others paint a more nuanced picture. For example, the British political economist David Ricardo* highlighted Smith's support for government protection of what are often called "infant industries."* These are economic entities that require protection before becoming fully established, but with the understanding that they will eventually be governed by the free market.[4]

Others question the portrayal of Smith as an advocate of free-market economics. As the American economist Herbert Stein* writes, "[Smith] was not pure or doctrinaire about this idea. He viewed government intervention in the market with great skepticism ... yet he was prepared to accept or propose qualifications to that policy in the specific cases where he judged that their net effect would be beneficial and would not undermine the basically free character of the system."[5]

The fact that these debates continue, and that all sides can find justification for their ideas, emphasizes the high level of complexity and nuance within Smith's work. Nevertheless, the strongest image of Smith is as the "founder of free-market economics." This image was created as a result of *The Wealth of Nations*.[6]

NOTES

1   List.co.uk, "100 Best Scottish Books: Adam Smith," accessed October 19, 2015, https://www.list.co.uk/articles/100-best-scottish-books/adam-smith/

2   BBC News, "Smith Replaces Elgar on £20 note," October 29, 2009, accessed October 19, 2015, http://news.bbc.co.uk/1/hi/business/6096938.stm

3   George J. Stigler, "The Successes and Failures of Professor Smith," *Journal of Political Economy*, 84, no. 6 (1976): 1202.

4   Christopher Zambakari, "Underdevelopment and Economic Theory of Growth: Case for Infant Industry Promotion," *Consilience: The Journal of Sustainable Development* 8, no. 1 (2012): 178.

5   Herbert Stein, "Board of Contributors: Remembering Adam Smith," *Wall Street Journal Asia*, April 6, 1994, A14.

6   P. J. O'Rourke, "Adam Smith: Web Junkie," *Forbes*, July 5, 2007, accessed October 19, 2015, http://www.forbes.com/free_forbes/2007/0507/086.html

MODULE 12
WHERE NEXT?

KEY POINTS

- *The Wealth of Nations* remains a key text in the study of economics.

- Scholars are arguing, increasingly, that it is incorrect to label Smith as a free-market ideologue. They point, instead, to arguments he made for greater government intervention in the sphere of social justice.

- Every economic participant in the world today operates in a world shaped by Smith's ideas.

Potential

Adam Smith's *The Wealth of Nations* will remain a key text in the study of economics. It is still the starting point in any debate on free-market economics.* The fact that there is still a clear divide between proponents of the free market and those who argue for a far more restricted and regulated form of capitalism* was highlighted by the global financial crisis of 2007–8* and the subsequent economic downturn. This led to increasing calls for capitalism to be regulated at the international level, as governments were forced to "bail out" private enterprises with taxpayers' funds.

In other areas the debates have moved on from the concerns of Smith's day. A key question now is how governments can reduce the massive inequalities that exist in free-market economies around the world. The level of interest in this topic is evidenced by the worldwide success of the recently published *Capital in the Twenty-First Century,* a book about inequality by the French economist Thomas Piketty.*[1]

> **❝ The reason that the invisible hand* often seems invisible is that it is often not there. ❞**
> Joseph E. Stiglitz,* 2014.

Many now question whether the current economic system is creating the conditions for free trade and markets that Smith would have advocated, or whether it is working against the conditions for growth in newly emerging economies. In *Kicking Away the Ladder: Development Strategy in Historical Perspective*, the South Korean economist Ha-Joon Chang asks: "How did the rich countries really become rich?" Chang argues that the developed world places great pressure on developing countries to adopt specific "good policies" and "good institutions," seen as necessary for economic development. However, adopting a historical approach, Chang argues that the economic evolution of now-developed countries followed none of the procedures that are being pushed on poorer nations. He concludes that developed countries are attempting to "kick away the ladder" with which they climbed to the top. They are preventing developing counties from adopting policies and utilizing institutions that they themselves used.[2]

Future Directions

Economists are split between those who credit Smith's writings with a free-market ideology, and those who pursue a more nuanced interpretation. One of the latter criticizes those who "slavishly followed the school of 'Free Trader'" for taking the teachings of Adam Smith at face value. He likens them to "the patient who followed a printed prescription and died of a misprint."[3]

Some contemporary policymakers are influenced by the work of the British economist John Maynard Keynes,* whose views ran counter to those of Smith. Following the onset of the 2007–8 financial crisis* the US President Barack Obama* steered a massive stimulus package through the United States Congress in order to boost employment and economic growth. At the other end of the American political spectrum, the "Tea Party"* wing of the Republican Party rejects any role for the government in managing the economy.

Increasingly, authors such as Ha-Joon Chang write of the Smithian "free-market" ideology as a means for countries such as Britain and the US to develop their economies, but then "kick away the ladder" for developing countries in Africa and elsewhere.[4] The Nobel Prize-winning American economist Joseph Stiglitz goes further. He argues that achieving global economic development will require a more nuanced understanding of "how we—the developed and developing countries, and the economies in transition—came to be where we are today."[5]

Summary

The importance of Smith's work is perhaps best summarized by the American economist and former US Federal Reserve* (central bank) chairman, Alan Greenspan:* "Without Smith's demonstration of the inherent stability and growth of what we now term free-market capitalism, the remarkable advance of material well-being for whole nations might well have been quashed. Pressures conceivably could have emerged to strengthen mercantilistic* regulations in response to the stresses created by competition and to the all-too-evident ills of industrialization."[6]

Economics remains split between economists who self-consciously follow Adam Smith and the classical* school of economics, and those who adhere to the Keynesian* tradition. Many of the specific issues under debate—such as how to define a "theory of value"* or the relative value of capital and labor—remain unresolved. Other lesser debates discuss issues of development and infant industries* (industries offered government capital and protection early in their development) in a free-market context. Whatever the outcome of these debates, the larger trend remains toward an ever more connected world, based on principles of freedom, free trade, and commerce. This is the world that Smith witnessed emerging. He sought to offer a systematic description of the dynamics underpinning it; the fact that his work continues to be considered relevant highlights his success.

NOTES

1   Thomas Piketty, *Capital In The Twenty-First Century* (Cambridge, MA: The Belknap Press Harvard University Press, 2014).

2   Ha-Joon Chang, *Kicking Away the Ladder: Development Strategy in Historical Perspective*, 1st ed. (London: Anthem Press, 2002).

3   Christopher Zambakari, "Underdevelopment and Economic Theory of Growth: Case for Infant Industry Promotion," *Consilience: The Journal of Sustainable Development*, 8, no. 1 (2012): 178.

4   Chang, *Kicking Away the Ladder*.

5   Zambakari, "Underdevelopment and Economic Theory," 179.

6   Alan Greenspan, "Remarks by Chairman Alan Greenspan: Adam Smith," The Federal Reserve Board, February 6, 2005, accessed October 19, 2015, http://www.federalreserve.gov/boarddocs/speeches/2005/20050206/default.htm

GLOSSARY

GLOSSARY OF TERMS

2007–8 Financial Crisis: widely considered the worst financial crisis since the Wall Street Crash of 1929.

Absolutism: form of government and political philosophy in which one person—such as a king, or other "absolute monarch"—holds all the power.

Aggregate demand: the total level of goods and services demanded in an economy at a given time. It consists of household spending on goods (C) + capital investments (I) + government spending (G) + exports (X) – (minus) imports from abroad (M). The standard equation is set out as $AD = C + I + G + (X - M)$.

Agrarianism: a philosophical tradition highlighting the greater value of agrarian life (life based around agriculture) relative to urban life.

Capitalism: an economic system in which industry and trade are controlled by private citizens with property rights over their goods and services. The forum in which trade takes place is the marketplace.

Classical economics: a theory that argues that market forces will lead the economy to equilibrium through the price mechanism that will efficiently allocate all available resources.

Communism: a form of government based on the anti-capitalist philosophy of Karl Marx, in which, theoretically, the ultimate aim is to establish a classless society where the means of production are communally owned by all citizens.

The Corn Laws: a set of laws that protected UK agriculture from 1815–46.

Demand: describes a consumer's desire and willingness to purchase a good or service.

Democratic Party: the major center-left party in the US political system.

Economic stagnation: a prolonged absence of economic growth.

Enlightenment: a period in Western political history when a new range of ideas and philosophy emerged, emphasizing individualism and freedom of thought.

Feudalism: a form of society and government in which—as in medieval Europe—society is rigidly stratified and status is based on land ownership.

Free-market economics: an economic philosophy that advocates minimal government intervention and individual freedom of action.

Full employment: a situation where all of those currently looking for employment are able to find it. Often approximated at 4 percent unemployment.

Global financial crisis 2007–8: a global economic downturn that is widely considered the worst financial crisis since the Great Depression of the 1930s.

Great Depression: the longest and most severe depression of the twentieth century. It originated in the US, with the collapse in stock prices in late 1929. Unemployment in the US reached 25 percent, while other countries saw it rise above 30 percent. In many countries, a prolonged recovery did not occur until the end of World War II.

Imperial federation: a proposal to turn the nineteenth-century British Empire from a collection of colonies with lower status than Britain itself into a single "federated" state in which they would have equal status with Britain.

Imperialism: a term for governmental policy that encourages the establishment of an empire beyond a country's borders—or, more generally, of expanding a country's influence abroad through military force, colonialism, or economic means.

Industrial Revolution: the period from the mid-eighteenth century to the mid-nineteenth century that saw the rapid expansion of new industrial manufacturing in Europe and America; it heralded a change from agrarian (farming-based) economies to urban and industrial economies.

Infant Industries: industries that are viewed as economically viable, for which the government provides capital and protection early in their development.

Inflation: the phenomenon of too much money chasing too few goods, causing a rise in the general price level.

Invisible hand: a descriptive tool used by economists to explain the outcome of markets, whereby the interaction between supply and demand produces stable market outcomes.

Keynesianism: a school of economic thought that argues that economic markets are not self-correcting. It suggests that proactive government policies can help to stabilize the economy through government spending (fiscal policy) and control of the supply of money (monetary policy).

Labor theory of value: an economic theory suggesting that the value of goods and services is determined by the labor required to produce them.

Laissez-faire: an economic system based on free trade and transactions between economic entities that are unfettered by government intervention.

Liberalism: a philosophy grounded in ideas of freedom and equality. It is generally viewed as consisting of two schools—classical liberalism, which places greater emphasis on liberty; and social liberalism, which places greater emphasis on equality.

Manchester School: a school of economic philosophy from nineteenth-century England that emphasized free trade and opposition to the Corn Laws.

Market economies: economies in which decisions are based on supply and demand.

Marxism: a political and economic ideology that pursues an analysis of class relations and conflict within society. It provides a critique of the development of capitalism and the role of class struggle in economic change.

Mercantilism: an economic regime practiced in Europe from the sixteenth to eighteenth centuries that forbade free trade between countries and encouraged governments to accumulate resources at the expense of their rivals. Adam Smith's *Wealth of Nations*, which argues for the benefits of free trade, was a rebuttal of this position.

Monetary policy: the mechanism used to control the supply of money. A policy that increases the money supply is generally described as expansionary while one that decreases the money supply is described as contractionary.

Monetarism: a set of policies based on free-market economics, which suggests that the role of the government is to keep tight control of the amount of money in circulation. Its most famous proponent was Milton Friedman.

Monopoly: A market where there is only one supplier who controls the price and output of the market.

Moral philosophy: the philosophical inquiry into the nature of ethics and ethical action.

Neoclassical Economics/Marginalism: a school of economics that constructs its understanding of markets and resource allocation based on three core assumptions: that people are rational and have discernible preferences based on value; that people maximize well-being while firms maximize profits; and that people have full and relevant information on which to act.

Philosophical Society of Edinburgh: a group that met to discuss recent developments and new ideas in the arts and sciences. Many of its members were academics employed at the University of Edinburgh.

Physiocracy: an economic theory developed in France during the eighteenth century, which suggested that national wealth was derived from agricultural wealth.

Political economy: before the development of the academic field of economics, "political economy" was the study of the economic operations of the "polity" (roughly, the state), considering things such as trade, labor, production, and national wealth.

Price mechanism: the way in which the market prices of commodities both reflect and affect the demand and supply of goods and services in the economy.

Protectionism: this is when a nation tries to protect its own producers and traders from competition from other nations. It might do so by imposing import taxes or subsidizing its own industries, for example.

Protestantism: a form of Christianity originating with the Protestant Reformation of the sixteenth century, in which various groups across Europe sought to break away from the Roman Catholic Church. Today, Protestants comprise almost 40 percent of Christians worldwide.

Resource allocation theory: The process through which an organization decides how to divide its resources between the activities in which it wishes to engage.

Reformation: A religious movement that occurred in Europe during the sixteenth century. Its followers (who eventually became known as Protestants) argued that people did not need religious leaders to interpret God's words. God's words were accessible to everyone through the Bible.

Roman Catholicism: the Roman Catholic Church is the largest and oldest of the Christian denominations. The head of the Catholic Church is the Pope, who resides in the Vatican in Italy. Approximately half of all Christians worldwide are Catholics.

Socialism: a political and economic system that aims for public ownership of the means of production.

Soviet Union, or USSR: a kind of "super state" that existed from 1922 to 1991, centered primarily on Russia and its neighbors in Eastern Europe and the northern half of Asia. It was the communist pole of the Cold War, with the United States as its main "rival."

Stagflation: a phenomenon in which economic stagnation occurs at the same time as rising prices (inflation).

Supply: the total amount of a specific good or service that is available to consumers.

Tea Party: a wing of the US Republican Party that advocates a minimalist role for government and a reduction in the societal tax burden.

US Federal Reserve: the central banking system and monetary authority in the United States.

World Trade Organization: a global international organization that deals with the rules of international trade.

World War II: global conflict from 1939 to 1945 that involved the world's great powers and numerous other countries around the globe.

Zero-sum game: a situation between two parties, in which a gain in well-being by one party results in a direct loss of well-being by the other.

PEOPLE MENTIONED IN THE TEXT

Thomas Aquinas (1225–74) was an Italian Dominican friar and philosopher who wrote about ethics and economics, discussing issues such as the division of labor, usury, and property rights.

Richard Cobden (1804–65) was an English industrialist and political radical. He became the leader of the free trade movement in the UK.

Jean-Baptiste Colbert (1619–83) was a French politician who served as minister of finance from 1665–83.

Milton Friedman (1912–2006) was an American economist. He was a recipient of the 1976 Nobel Memorial Prize in Economic Sciences. He is considered one of the most influential economists of the twentieth century.

Edward Gibbon (1737–94) was an English Member of Parliament and one of the most important historians on the subject of the Roman Empire.

Alan Greenspan (b. 1926) is the former chairman of the US Federal Reserve.

Alexander Hamilton (1755–1804) was a founding father of the United States and served as the country's first secretary of the treasury (finance minister).

Friedrich von Hayek (1899–1992) was an Austrian and British economist best known for his work defending classical liberalism.

David Hume (1711–76) was a Scottish intellectual who focused on philosophy, history, and economics.

Francis Hutcheson (1694–1746) was a Scottish philosopher and is considered one of the founders of the Scottish Enlightenment.

Thomas Jefferson (1743–1826) was a founding father and third president of the United States of America.

John Maynard Keynes (1883–1946) was a Cambridge-based British economist who transformed the study of economics.

Paul Krugman (b. 1953) is an American economist and a professor of economics and international affairs at Princeton University.

Karl Marx (1818–83) was a revolutionary German thinker, philosopher, economist, sociologist, and historian. Author of *The Communist Manifesto* and *Capital*, his theories focused on the relationship between labor and capital, and gave rise to Marxism.

John Stuart Mill (1806–73) was a British philosopher and political economist who advocated individual freedom. He was one of the most influential proponents of liberalism, a political philosophy based on the ideas of liberty and equality.

Richard Nixon (1913–1994) was the 37th president of the United States, who served from 1969–74.

Barack Obama (b. 1961) is the 44th president of the United States.

Thomas Piketty (b. 1971) is a French economist who is best known for his work on inequality.

François Quesnay (1694–1774) was a French economist and one of the leading members of the physiocratic school.

Ronald Reagan (1911–2004) was the 40th president of the United States and a strong proponent of free markets.

David Ricardo (1772–1823) was an influential British political economist. Author of "On the Principles of Political Economy and Taxation," he argued in favor of free-market policies and was the founder of classical economics, also known as Ricardian economics, together with James Mill.

Joseph Schumpeter (1883–1950) was an Austrian American economist. He served as Austria's finance minister in 1919 and eventually moved to Harvard University.

Herbert Stein (1916–99) was an American economist who served at the American Enterprise Institute and worked with the *Wall Street Journal*.

George Stigler (1911–91) was an American economist who served as president of the American Economic Association. He won the Nobel Prize in Economic Science in 1982.

Joseph E. Stiglitz (b. 1943) is an American economist who served as chief economist of the World Bank. He is a Nobel Laureate in economics.

Margaret Thatcher (1925–2013) was prime minister of the United Kingdom from 1975–90. She is widely viewed as having been a champion of free-market ideology.

Voltaire (1694–1778) was the pseudonym of François-Marie Arouet, a French Enlightenment writer and philosopher who advocated, among other things, the rights of the individual and the separation of Church and state.

WORKS CITED

WORKS CITED

BBC News. "Smith Replaces Elgar on £20 note." October 29, 2006. Accessed October 16, 2015. http://news.bbc.co.uk/1/hi/business/6096938.stm

Benians, E. A. "Adam Smith's Project of an Empire." *Cambridge Historical Journal I* (1925): 249–283.

Buchan, James. *The Authentic Adam Smith: His Life and Ideas*. New York: W. W. Norton & Company, 2006.

Buchholz, Todd. *New Ideas from Dead Economists: An Introduction to Modern Economic Thought*. London: Penguin Books, 1999.

Bussing-Burks, Marie. *Influential Economists*. Minneapolis: The Oliver Press, 2003.

Campos, Antonietta. "Marginalist Economics." *The New Palgrave: A Dictionary of Economics, Volume III*. London: MacMillan, 1987.

Cassidy, John. "The Demand Doctor." *The New Yorker*. October 10, 2011. Accessed October 26, 2015. http://www.newyorker.com/magazine/2011/10/10/the-demand-doctor

Chang, Ha-Joon. *Kicking Away the Ladder: Development Strategy in Historical Perspective*. 1st edition. London: Anthem Press, 2002.

Ekelund, R. and R. Hebert. *A History of Economic Theory and Method*, 5thedition. Long Grove, IL: Waveland Press, 2007.

Fleischacker, Samuel. *On Adam Smith's "Wealth of Nations": A Philosophical Companion*. Princeton, NJ: Princeton University Press, 2004.

Friedman, Milton. "The Role of Monetary Policy." *American Economic Review* 58, no. 1 (1968): 1–17.

Friedman, Milton, and Rose D. Friedman. *Capitalism and Freedom*. 40th edition. Chicago, IL: University of Chicago Press, 2002.

Fukuyama, Francis. *The End of History and the Last Man*. 1st editon. New York: Maxwell Macmillan International, 1992.

Greenspan, Alan. "Remarks by Chairman Alan Greenspan: Adam Smith." The Federal Reserve Board. February 6, 2005. Accessed October 16, 2015. http://www.federalreserve.gov/boarddocs/speeches/2005/20050206/default.htm

Hayek, F. A. *The Road to Serfdom*. Chicago: University of Chicago Press, 1994.

Hume, David. *A Treatise on Human Nature*. New York: HarperTorch, 2014.

Irwin, Douglas A.. "The Aftermath of Hamilton's 'Report on Manufactures'." *Journal of Economic History* 64, no. 3 (2004): 800–821.

Jefferson, Thomas. *Writings*. New York: Library of America, 1984.

Jevons, W. Stanley. *The Theory of Political Economy*. 2nd edition. London: MacMillian,1879.

Keynes, John Maynard. *The End of Laissez-Faire*. New York: Prometheus Books, 2004.

The General Theory of Employment, Interest and Money. Vol. 7, *The Collected Writings of John Maynard Keynes.* London: Macmillan St. Martin's Press, 1973.

Krugman, Paul. "Plutocracy, Paralysis, Perplexity." *New York Times*. May 3, 2012.

End This Depression Now! New York: W. W. Norton & Co, 2013.

Levy, David M. and Sandra J. Peart. "The Secret History of the Dismal Science. Part I. Economics, Religion and Race in the 19th Century." *Library of Economics and Liberty*. January 22, 2001. Accessed October 16, 2015. http://www.econlib.org/library/Columns/LevyPeartdismal.html

List.co.uk. "100 Best Scottish Books: Adam Smith." Accessed October 16, 2015. https://www.list.co.uk/articles/100-best-scottish-books/adam-smith/

Martin, Christopher. "Adam Smith and Liberal Economics: Reading the Minimum Wage Debate of 1795–96." *Econ Journal Watch* 8, no. 2 (May 2011): 110–25.

McCusker, John J. *Mercantilism and the Economic History of the Early Modern Atlantic World*. Cambridge: Cambridge University Press, 2001.

Nester, R. *The Great Frontier War: Britain, France, and the Imperial Struggle for North America, 1607–1755*. Westport, Conn: Praeger, 2000.

O'Rourke, P.J. "Adam Smith: Web Junkie." *Forbes*. July 5, 2007. Accessed October 16, 2015. http://www.forbes.com/free_forbes/2007/0507/086.html

Pack, Spencer J. *Capitalism as a Moral System: Adam Smith's Critique of the Free Market Economy*. Aldershot: Edward Elgar, 2010.

Palen, Marc-William. "Adam Smith as Advocate of Empire, c. 1870–1932." *Historical Journal* 57, no. 1 (2014): 179–98.

Piketty, Thomas. *Capital in the Twenty-First Century*. Cambridge, MA: The Belknap Press, Harvard University Press, 2014.

Rae, John. *Life of Adam Smith*. London & New York: Macmillan, 1895.

Robbins, Lionel. *A History of Economic Thought*. Princeton: Princeton University Press, 1998.

Robinson, Joan. *Economic Philosophy*. Piscataway, NJ: Transaction Publishers, 2006.

Schumpeter, Joseph. *History of Economic Analysis*. New York: Oxford University Press, 1996.

Scott, W. R. "The Never to Be Forgotten Hutcheson: Excerpts from W. R. Scott." *Econ Journal Watch* 8, no. 1 (January 2011): 96–109.

Seabrooke, L. *Global Standards of Market Civilization*. London: Taylor & Francis, 2006.

Smith, Adam. *An Inquiry into the Nature and Causes of the Wealth of Nations: Books I, II, III, IV and V*. New York: Metalibri Digital Edition, 2007. Accessed October 16, 2015. http://www.ibiblio.org/ml/libri/s/SmithA_WealthNations_p.pdf

The Theory of Moral Sentiments. Edited by Knud Haakonssen. Cambridge: Cambridge University Press, 2002.

Snowdon, Brian, and Howard R. Vane. *Modern Macroeconomics: Its Origins, Development and Current State*. 1st edition. Cheltenham: Edward Elgar Publishing, 2005.

Stein, Herbert. "Board of Contributors: Remembering Adam Smith." *The Wall Street Journal Asia*. April 6, 1994.

Steiner, Phillippe. "Physiocracy and French Pre-Classical Political Economy." In *A Companion to the History of Economic Thought*, edited by Jeff E. Biddle, Jon B. Davis, and Warren Samuels. Oxford: Blackwell Publishing, 2003.

Stigler, George. "The Successes and Failures of Professor Smith." *Journal of Political Economy* 84, no. 6 (1976): 1199–213.

Viner, Jacob and Douglas A. Irwin, ed. *Essays on the Intellectual History of Economics*. Princeton, NJ: Princeton University Press, 1991.

Winch, Donald. "Smith, Adam." *Dictionary of National Biography*. Oxford: Oxford University Press, 2004.

Christopher Zambakari. "Underdevelopment and Economic Theory of Growth: Case for Infant Industry Promotion." *Consilience: The Journal of Sustainable Development* 8, no. 1 (2012): 171–87.

THE MACAT LIBRARY
BY DISCIPLINE

AFRICANA STUDIES

Chinua Achebe's *An Image of Africa: Racism in Conrad's Heart of Darkness*
W. E. B. Du Bois's *The Souls of Black Folk*
Zora Neale Huston's *Characteristics of Negro Expression*
Martin Luther King Jr's *Why We Can't Wait*
Toni Morrison's *Playing in the Dark: Whiteness in the American Literary Imagination*

ANTHROPOLOGY

Arjun Appadurai's *Modernity at Large: Cultural Dimensions of Globalisation*
Philippe Ariès's *Centuries of Childhood*
Franz Boas's *Race, Language and Culture*
Kim Chan & Renée Mauborgne's *Blue Ocean Strategy*
Jared Diamond's *Guns, Germs & Steel: the Fate of Human Societies*
Jared Diamond's *Collapse: How Societies Choose to Fail or Survive*
E. E. Evans-Pritchard's *Witchcraft, Oracles and Magic Among the Azande*
James Ferguson's *The Anti-Politics Machine*
Clifford Geertz's *The Interpretation of Cultures*
David Graeber's *Debt: the First 5000 Years*
Karen Ho's *Liquidated: An Ethnography of Wall Street*
Geert Hofstede's *Culture's Consequences: Comparing Values, Behaviors, Institutes and Organizations across Nations*
Claude Lévi-Strauss's *Structural Anthropology*
Jay Macleod's *Ain't No Makin' It: Aspirations and Attainment in a Low-Income Neighborhood*
Saba Mahmood's *The Politics of Piety: The Islamic Revival and the Feminist Subject*
Marcel Mauss's *The Gift*

BUSINESS

Jean Lave & Etienne Wenger's *Situated Learning*
Theodore Levitt's *Marketing Myopia*
Burton G. Malkiel's *A Random Walk Down Wall Street*
Douglas McGregor's *The Human Side of Enterprise*
Michael Porter's *Competitive Strategy: Creating and Sustaining Superior Performance*
John Kotter's *Leading Change*
C. K. Prahalad & Gary Hamel's *The Core Competence of the Corporation*

CRIMINOLOGY

Michelle Alexander's *The New Jim Crow: Mass Incarceration in the Age of Colorblindness*
Michael R. Gottfredson & Travis Hirschi's *A General Theory of Crime*
Richard Herrnstein & Charles A. Murray's *The Bell Curve: Intelligence and Class Structure in American Life*
Elizabeth Loftus's *Eyewitness Testimony*
Jay Macleod's *Ain't No Makin' It: Aspirations and Attainment in a Low-Income Neighborhood*
Philip Zimbardo's *The Lucifer Effect*

ECONOMICS

Janet Abu-Lughod's *Before European Hegemony*
Ha-Joon Chang's *Kicking Away the Ladder*
David Brion Davis's *The Problem of Slavery in the Age of Revolution*
Milton Friedman's *The Role of Monetary Policy*
Milton Friedman's *Capitalism and Freedom*
David Graeber's *Debt: the First 5000 Years*
Friedrich Hayek's *The Road to Serfdom*
Karen Ho's *Liquidated: An Ethnography of Wall Street*

John Maynard Keynes's *The General Theory of Employment, Interest and Money*
Charles P. Kindleberger's *Manias, Panics and Crashes*
Robert Lucas's *Why Doesn't Capital Flow from Rich to Poor Countries?*
Burton G. Malkiel's *A Random Walk Down Wall Street*
Thomas Robert Malthus's *An Essay on the Principle of Population*
Karl Marx's *Capital*
Thomas Piketty's *Capital in the Twenty-First Century*
Amartya Sen's *Development as Freedom*
Adam Smith's *The Wealth of Nations*
Nassim Nicholas Taleb's *The Black Swan: The Impact of the Highly Improbable*
Amos Tversky's & Daniel Kahneman's *Judgment under Uncertainty: Heuristics and Biases*
Mahbub Ul Haq's *Reflections on Human Development*
Max Weber's *The Protestant Ethic and the Spirit of Capitalism*

FEMINISM AND GENDER STUDIES

Judith Butler's *Gender Trouble*
Simone De Beauvoir's *The Second Sex*
Michel Foucault's *History of Sexuality*
Betty Friedan's *The Feminine Mystique*
Saba Mahmood's *The Politics of Piety: The Islamic Revival and the Feminist Subject*
Joan Wallach Scott's *Gender and the Politics of History*
Mary Wollstonecraft's *A Vindication of the Rights of Woman*
Virginia Woolf's *A Room of One's Own*

GEOGRAPHY

The Brundtland Report's *Our Common Future*
Rachel Carson's *Silent Spring*
Charles Darwin's *On the Origin of Species*
James Ferguson's *The Anti-Politics Machine*
Jane Jacobs's *The Death and Life of Great American Cities*
James Lovelock's *Gaia: A New Look at Life on Earth*
Amartya Sen's *Development as Freedom*
Mathis Wackernagel & William Rees's *Our Ecological Footprint*

HISTORY

Janet Abu-Lughod's *Before European Hegemony*
Benedict Anderson's *Imagined Communities*
Bernard Bailyn's *The Ideological Origins of the American Revolution*
Hanna Batatu's *The Old Social Classes And The Revolutionary Movements Of Iraq*
Christopher Browning's *Ordinary Men: Reserve Police Batallion 101 and the Final Solution in Poland*
Edmund Burke's *Reflections on the Revolution in France*
William Cronon's *Nature's Metropolis: Chicago And The Great West*
Alfred W. Crosby's *The Columbian Exchange*
Hamid Dabashi's *Iran: A People Interrupted*
David Brion Davis's *The Problem of Slavery in the Age of Revolution*
Nathalie Zemon Davis's *The Return of Martin Guerre*
Jared Diamond's *Guns, Germs & Steel: the Fate of Human Societies*
Frank Dikotter's *Mao's Great Famine*
John W Dower's *War Without Mercy: Race And Power In The Pacific War*
W. E. B. Du Bois's *The Souls of Black Folk*
Richard J. Evans's *In Defence of History*
Lucien Febvre's *The Problem of Unbelief in the 16th Century*
Sheila Fitzpatrick's *Everyday Stalinism*

Eric Foner's *Reconstruction: America's Unfinished Revolution, 1863-1877*
Michel Foucault's *Discipline and Punish*
Michel Foucault's *History of Sexuality*
Francis Fukuyama's *The End of History and the Last Man*
John Lewis Gaddis's *We Now Know: Rethinking Cold War History*
Ernest Gellner's *Nations and Nationalism*
Eugene Genovese's *Roll, Jordan, Roll: The World the Slaves Made*
Carlo Ginzburg's *The Night Battles*
Daniel Goldhagen's *Hitler's Willing Executioners*
Jack Goldstone's *Revolution and Rebellion in the Early Modern World*
Antonio Gramsci's *The Prison Notebooks*
Alexander Hamilton, John Jay & James Madison's *The Federalist Papers*
Christopher Hill's *The World Turned Upside Down*
Carole Hillenbrand's *The Crusades: Islamic Perspectives*
Thomas Hobbes's *Leviathan*
Eric Hobsbawm's *The Age Of Revolution*
John A. Hobson's *Imperialism: A Study*
Albert Hourani's *History of the Arab Peoples*
Samuel P. Huntington's *The Clash of Civilizations and the Remaking of World Order*
C. L. R. James's *The Black Jacobins*
Tony Judt's *Postwar: A History of Europe Since 1945*
Ernst Kantorowicz's *The King's Two Bodies: A Study in Medieval Political Theology*
Paul Kennedy's *The Rise and Fall of the Great Powers*
Ian Kershaw's *The "Hitler Myth": Image and Reality in the Third Reich*
John Maynard Keynes's *The General Theory of Employment, Interest and Money*
Charles P. Kindleberger's *Manias, Panics and Crashes*
Martin Luther King Jr's *Why We Can't Wait*
Henry Kissinger's *World Order: Reflections on the Character of Nations and the Course of History*
Thomas Kuhn's *The Structure of Scientific Revolutions*
Georges Lefebvre's *The Coming of the French Revolution*
John Locke's *Two Treatises of Government*
Niccolò Machiavelli's *The Prince*
Thomas Robert Malthus's *An Essay on the Principle of Population*
Mahmood Mamdani's *Citizen and Subject: Contemporary Africa And The Legacy Of Late Colonialism*
Karl Marx's *Capital*
Stanley Milgram's *Obedience to Authority*
John Stuart Mill's *On Liberty*
Thomas Paine's *Common Sense*
Thomas Paine's *Rights of Man*
Geoffrey Parker's *Global Crisis: War, Climate Change and Catastrophe in the Seventeenth Century*
Jonathan Riley-Smith's *The First Crusade and the Idea of Crusading*
Jean-Jacques Rousseau's *The Social Contract*
Joan Wallach Scott's *Gender and the Politics of History*
Theda Skocpol's *States and Social Revolutions*
Adam Smith's *The Wealth of Nations*
Timothy Snyder's *Bloodlands: Europe Between Hitler and Stalin*
Sun Tzu's *The Art of War*
Keith Thomas's *Religion and the Decline of Magic*
Thucydides's *The History of the Peloponnesian War*
Frederick Jackson Turner's *The Significance of the Frontier in American History*
Odd Arne Westad's *The Global Cold War: Third World Interventions And The Making Of Our Times*

LITERATURE

Chinua Achebe's *An Image of Africa: Racism in Conrad's Heart of Darkness*
Roland Barthes's *Mythologies*
Homi K. Bhabha's *The Location of Culture*
Judith Butler's *Gender Trouble*
Simone De Beauvoir's *The Second Sex*
Ferdinand De Saussure's *Course in General Linguistics*
T. S. Eliot's *The Sacred Wood: Essays on Poetry and Criticism*
Zora Neale Huston's *Characteristics of Negro Expression*
Toni Morrison's *Playing in the Dark: Whiteness in the American Literary Imagination*
Edward Said's *Orientalism*
Gayatri Chakravorty Spivak's *Can the Subaltern Speak?*
Mary Wollstonecraft's *A Vindication of the Rights of Women*
Virginia Woolf's *A Room of One's Own*

PHILOSOPHY

Elizabeth Anscombe's *Modern Moral Philosophy*
Hannah Arendt's *The Human Condition*
Aristotle's *Metaphysics*
Aristotle's *Nicomachean Ethics*
Edmund Gettier's *Is Justified True Belief Knowledge?*
Georg Wilhelm Friedrich Hegel's *Phenomenology of Spirit*
David Hume's *Dialogues Concerning Natural Religion*
David Hume's *The Enquiry for Human Understanding*
Immanuel Kant's *Religion within the Boundaries of Mere Reason*
Immanuel Kant's *Critique of Pure Reason*
Søren Kierkegaard's *The Sickness Unto Death*
Søren Kierkegaard's *Fear and Trembling*
C. S. Lewis's *The Abolition of Man*
Alasdair MacIntyre's *After Virtue*
Marcus Aurelius's *Meditations*
Friedrich Nietzsche's *On the Genealogy of Morality*
Friedrich Nietzsche's *Beyond Good and Evil*
Plato's *Republic*
Plato's *Symposium*
Jean-Jacques Rousseau's *The Social Contract*
Gilbert Ryle's *The Concept of Mind*
Baruch Spinoza's *Ethics*
Sun Tzu's *The Art of War*
Ludwig Wittgenstein's *Philosophical Investigations*

POLITICS

Benedict Anderson's *Imagined Communities*
Aristotle's *Politics*
Bernard Bailyn's *The Ideological Origins of the American Revolution*
Edmund Burke's *Reflections on the Revolution in France*
John C. Calhoun's *A Disquisition on Government*
Ha-Joon Chang's *Kicking Away the Ladder*
Hamid Dabashi's *Iran: A People Interrupted*
Hamid Dabashi's *Theology of Discontent: The Ideological Foundation of the Islamic Revolution in Iran*
Robert Dahl's *Democracy and its Critics*
Robert Dahl's *Who Governs?*
David Brion Davis's *The Problem of Slavery in the Age of Revolution*

Alexis De Tocqueville's *Democracy in America*
James Ferguson's *The Anti-Politics Machine*
Frank Dikotter's *Mao's Great Famine*
Sheila Fitzpatrick's *Everyday Stalinism*
Eric Foner's *Reconstruction: America's Unfinished Revolution, 1863-1877*
Milton Friedman's *Capitalism and Freedom*
Francis Fukuyama's *The End of History and the Last Man*
John Lewis Gaddis's *We Now Know: Rethinking Cold War History*
Ernest Gellner's *Nations and Nationalism*
David Graeber's *Debt: the First 5000 Years*
Antonio Gramsci's *The Prison Notebooks*
Alexander Hamilton, John Jay & James Madison's *The Federalist Papers*
Friedrich Hayek's *The Road to Serfdom*
Christopher Hill's *The World Turned Upside Down*
Thomas Hobbes's *Leviathan*
John A. Hobson's *Imperialism: A Study*
Samuel P. Huntington's *The Clash of Civilizations and the Remaking of World Order*
Tony Judt's *Postwar: A History of Europe Since 1945*
David C. Kang's *China Rising: Peace, Power and Order in East Asia*
Paul Kennedy's *The Rise and Fall of Great Powers*
Robert Keohane's *After Hegemony*
Martin Luther King Jr.'s *Why We Can't Wait*
Henry Kissinger's *World Order: Reflections on the Character of Nations and the Course of History*
John Locke's *Two Treatises of Government*
Niccolò Machiavelli's *The Prince*
Thomas Robert Malthus's *An Essay on the Principle of Population*
Mahmood Mamdani's *Citizen and Subject: Contemporary Africa And The Legacy Of Late Colonialism*
Karl Marx's *Capital*
John Stuart Mill's *On Liberty*
John Stuart Mill's *Utilitarianism*
Hans Morgenthau's *Politics Among Nations*
Thomas Paine's *Common Sense*
Thomas Paine's *Rights of Man*
Thomas Piketty's *Capital in the Twenty-First Century*
Robert D. Putman's *Bowling Alone*
John Rawls's *Theory of Justice*
Jean-Jacques Rousseau's *The Social Contract*
Theda Skocpol's *States and Social Revolutions*
Adam Smith's *The Wealth of Nations*
Sun Tzu's *The Art of War*
Henry David Thoreau's *Civil Disobedience*
Thucydides's *The History of the Peloponnesian War*
Kenneth Waltz's *Theory of International Politics*
Max Weber's *Politics as a Vocation*
Odd Arne Westad's *The Global Cold War: Third World Interventions And The Making Of Our Times*

POSTCOLONIAL STUDIES

Roland Barthes's *Mythologies*
Frantz Fanon's *Black Skin, White Masks*
Homi K. Bhabha's *The Location of Culture*
Gustavo Gutiérrez's *A Theology of Liberation*
Edward Said's *Orientalism*
Gayatri Chakravorty Spivak's *Can the Subaltern Speak?*

PSYCHOLOGY

Gordon Allport's *The Nature of Prejudice*
Alan Baddeley & Graham Hitch's *Aggression: A Social Learning Analysis*
Albert Bandura's *Aggression: A Social Learning Analysis*
Leon Festinger's *A Theory of Cognitive Dissonance*
Sigmund Freud's *The Interpretation of Dreams*
Betty Friedan's *The Feminine Mystique*
Michael R. Gottfredson & Travis Hirschi's *A General Theory of Crime*
Eric Hoffer's *The True Believer: Thoughts on the Nature of Mass Movements*
William James's *Principles of Psychology*
Elizabeth Loftus's *Eyewitness Testimony*
A. H. Maslow's *A Theory of Human Motivation*
Stanley Milgram's *Obedience to Authority*
Steven Pinker's *The Better Angels of Our Nature*
Oliver Sacks's *The Man Who Mistook His Wife For a Hat*
Richard Thaler & Cass Sunstein's *Nudge: Improving Decisions About Health, Wealth and Happiness*
Amos Tversky's *Judgment under Uncertainty: Heuristics and Biases*
Philip Zimbardo's *The Lucifer Effect*

SCIENCE

Rachel Carson's *Silent Spring*
William Cronon's *Nature's Metropolis: Chicago And The Great West*
Alfred W. Crosby's *The Columbian Exchange*
Charles Darwin's *On the Origin of Species*
Richard Dawkin's *The Selfish Gene*
Thomas Kuhn's *The Structure of Scientific Revolutions*
Geoffrey Parker's *Global Crisis: War, Climate Change and Catastrophe in the Seventeenth Century*
Mathis Wackernagel & William Rees's *Our Ecological Footprint*

SOCIOLOGY

Michelle Alexander's *The New Jim Crow: Mass Incarceration in the Age of Colorblindness*
Gordon Allport's *The Nature of Prejudice*
Albert Bandura's *Aggression: A Social Learning Analysis*
Hanna Batatu's *The Old Social Classes And The Revolutionary Movements Of Iraq*
Ha-Joon Chang's *Kicking Away the Ladder*
W. E. B. Du Bois's *The Souls of Black Folk*
Émile Durkheim's *On Suicide*
Frantz Fanon's *Black Skin, White Masks*
Frantz Fanon's *The Wretched of the Earth*
Eric Foner's *Reconstruction: America's Unfinished Revolution, 1863-1877*
Eugene Genovese's *Roll, Jordan, Roll: The World the Slaves Made*
Jack Goldstone's *Revolution and Rebellion in the Early Modern World*
Antonio Gramsci's *The Prison Notebooks*
Richard Herrnstein & Charles A Murray's *The Bell Curve: Intelligence and Class Structure in American Life*
Eric Hoffer's *The True Believer: Thoughts on the Nature of Mass Movements*
Jane Jacobs's *The Death and Life of Great American Cities*
Robert Lucas's *Why Doesn't Capital Flow from Rich to Poor Countries?*
Jay Macleod's *Ain't No Makin' It: Aspirations and Attainment in a Low Income Neighborhood*
Elaine May's *Homeward Bound: American Families in the Cold War Era*
Douglas McGregor's *The Human Side of Enterprise*
C. Wright Mills's *The Sociological Imagination*

Thomas Piketty's *Capital in the Twenty-First Century*
Robert D. Putman's *Bowling Alone*
David Riesman's *The Lonely Crowd: A Study of the Changing American Character*
Edward Said's *Orientalism*
Joan Wallach Scott's *Gender and the Politics of History*
Theda Skocpol's *States and Social Revolutions*
Max Weber's *The Protestant Ethic and the Spirit of Capitalism*

THEOLOGY

Augustine's *Confessions*
Benedict's *Rule of St Benedict*
Gustavo Gutiérrez's *A Theology of Liberation*
Carole Hillenbrand's *The Crusades: Islamic Perspectives*
David Hume's *Dialogues Concerning Natural Religion*
Immanuel Kant's *Religion within the Boundaries of Mere Reason*
Ernst Kantorowicz's *The King's Two Bodies: A Study in Medieval Political Theology*
Søren Kierkegaard's *The Sickness Unto Death*
C. S. Lewis's *The Abolition of Man*
Saba Mahmood's *The Politics of Piety: The Islamic Revival and the Feminist Subject*
Baruch Spinoza's *Ethics*
Keith Thomas's *Religion and the Decline of Magic*

COMING SOON

Chris Argyris's *The Individual and the Organisation*
Seyla Benhabib's *The Rights of Others*
Walter Benjamin's *The Work Of Art in the Age of Mechanical Reproduction*
John Berger's *Ways of Seeing*
Pierre Bourdieu's *Outline of a Theory of Practice*
Mary Douglas's *Purity and Danger*
Roland Dworkin's *Taking Rights Seriously*
James G. March's *Exploration and Exploitation in Organisational Learning*
Ikujiro Nonaka's *A Dynamic Theory of Organizational Knowledge Creation*
Griselda Pollock's *Vision and Difference*
Amartya Sen's *Inequality Re-Examined*
Susan Sontag's *On Photography*
Yasser Tabbaa's *The Transformation of Islamic Art*
Ludwig von Mises's *Theory of Money and Credit*

Macat Disciplines

Access the greatest ideas and thinkers across entire disciplines, including

Postcolonial Studies

Roland Barthes's *Mythologies*
Frantz Fanon's *Black Skin, White Masks*
Homi K. Bhabha's *The Location of Culture*
Gustavo Gutiérrez's *A Theology of Liberation*
Edward Said's *Orientalism*
Gayatri Chakravorty Spivak's *Can the Subaltern Speak?*

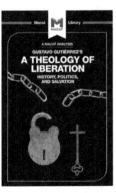

Macat analyses are available from all good bookshops and libraries.

Access hundreds of analyses through one, multimedia tool.
Join free for one month **library.macat.com**

Macat Disciplines

Access the greatest ideas and thinkers across entire disciplines, including

CRIMINOLOGY

Michelle Alexander's
The New Jim Crow: Mass Incarceration in the Age of Colorblindness

Michael R. Gottfredson & Travis Hirschi's
A General Theory of Crime

Elizabeth Loftus's
Eyewitness Testimony

Richard Herrnstein & Charles A. Murray's
The Bell Curve: Intelligence and Class Structure in American Life

Jay Macleod's
Ain't No Makin' It: Aspirations and Attainment in a Low-Income Neighborhood

Philip Zimbardo's
The Lucifer Effect

Macat analyses are available from all good bookshops and libraries.

Access hundreds of analyses through one, multimedia tool.
Join free for one month **library.macat.com**

Macat Disciplines

Access the greatest ideas and thinkers across entire disciplines, including

INEQUALITY

Ha-Joon Chang's, *Kicking Away the Ladder*

David Graeber's, *Debt: The First 5000 Years*

Robert E. Lucas's, *Why Doesn't Capital Flow from Rich To Poor Countries?*

Thomas Piketty's, *Capital in the Twenty-First Century*

Amartya Sen's, *Inequality Re-Examined*

Mahbub Ul Haq's, *Reflections on Human Development*

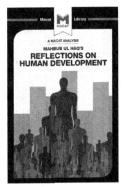

Macat analyses are available from all good bookshops and libraries.

Access hundreds of analyses through one, multimedia tool.
Join free for one month **library.macat.com**

MACAT

Macat Pairs

Analyse historical and modern issues from opposite sides of an argument. Pairs include:

MACAT

HOW TO RUN AN ECONOMY

John Maynard Keynes's
The General Theory OF Employment, Interest and Money

Classical economics suggests that market economies are self-correcting in times of recession or depression, and tend toward full employment and output. But English economist John Maynard Keynes disagrees.

In his ground-breaking 1936 study *The General Theory*, Keynes argues that traditional economics has misunderstood the causes of unemployment. Employment is not determined by the price of labor; it is directly linked to demand. Keynes believes market economies are by nature unstable, and so require government intervention. Spurred on by the social catastrophe of the Great Depression of the 1930s, he sets out to revolutionize the way the world thinks

Milton Friedman's
The Role of Monetary Policy

Friedman's 1968 paper changed the course of economic theory. In just 17 pages, he demolished existing theory and outlined an effective alternate monetary policy designed to secure 'high employment, stable prices and rapid growth.'

Friedman demonstrated that monetary policy plays a vital role in broader economic stability and argued that economists got their monetary policy wrong in the 1950s and 1960s by misunderstanding the relationship between inflation and unemployment. Previous generations of economists had believed that governments could permanently decrease unemployment by permitting inflation—and vice versa. Friedman's most original contribution was to show that this supposed trade-off is an illusion that only works in the short term.

Macat analyses are available from all good bookshops and libraries.

Access hundreds of analyses through one, multimedia tool.
Join free for one month **library.macat.com**

Macat Pairs

Analyse historical and modern issues from opposite sides of an argument. Pairs include:

ARE WE FUNDAMENTALLY GOOD - OR BAD?

Steven Pinker's
The Better Angels of Our Nature

Stephen Pinker's gloriously optimistic 2011 book argues that, despite humanity's biological tendency toward violence, we are, in fact, less violent today than ever before. To prove his case, Pinker lays out pages of detailed statistical evidence. For him, much of the credit for the decline goes to the eighteenth-century Enlightenment movement, whose ideas of liberty, tolerance, and respect for the value of human life filtered down through society and affected how people thought. That psychological change led to behavioral change—and overall we became more peaceful. Critics countered that humanity could never overcome the biological urge toward violence; others argued that Pinker's statistics were flawed.

Philip Zimbardo's
The Lucifer Effect

Some psychologists believe those who commit cruelty are innately evil. Zimbardo disagrees. In *The Lucifer Effect*, he argues that sometimes good people do evil things simply because of the situations they find themselves in, citing many historical examples to illustrate his point. Zimbardo details his 1971 Stanford prison experiment, where ordinary volunteers playing guards in a mock prison rapidly became abusive. But he also describes the tortures committed by US army personnel in Iraq's Abu Ghraib prison in 2003—and how he himself testified in defence of one of those guards. committed by US army personnel in Iraq's Abu Ghraib prison in 2003—and how he himself testified in defence of one of those guards.

Macat analyses are available from all good bookshops and libraries.

Access hundreds of analyses through one, multimedia tool.
Join free for one month **library.macat.com**

Printed in the United States
by Baker & Taylor Publisher Services